P9-BZQ-729

WITHDRAWN

EX LIBRIS

1961

IN A DEMOCRACY EDUCATIONAL OPPORTUNITY FOR ALL

Everett Baker
Learning Resources Center
NORWALK COMMUNITY COLLEGE

STAR WARS

The Strategic Defense Initiative Debates in Congress

Senator Larry Pressler

Everett Baker
Learning Resources Center
NORWALK COMMUNITY COLLEGE

PRAEGER

PRAEGER SPECIAL STUDIES • PRAEGER SCIENTIFIC
New York • Westport, Connecticut • London

Library of Congress Cataloging-in-Publication Data

Pressler, Larry, 1942-
    Star Wars: the Strategic Defense Initiative
debates in Congress.

    Bibliography: p.
    Includes index.
    1. Strategic Defense Initiative. I. Title.
UG743.P75   1986   358'.1754   86-809
ISBN 0-275-92052-6 (alk. paper)

Copyright © 1986 by Praeger Publishers

All rights reserved. No portion of this book may be reproduced, by
any process or technique, without the express written consent of
the publisher.

Library of Congress Catalog Card Number: 86-809
ISBN: 0-275-92052-6

First published in 1986

Praeger Publishers, 521 Fifth Avenue, New York, NY 10175
A division of Greenwood Press, Inc.

Printed in the United States of America

The paper used in this book complies with the Permanent Paper
Standard issued by the National Information Standards Organization (Z39.48-1984).

10   9   8   7   6   5   4   3   2   1

Foreword

While predictions about the future should normally be treated with wariness, one aspect of the nation's policy debates can now be stated with high confidence. For the foreseeable future the discussion of both foreign and defense policy will be strongly influenced, indeed regularly dominated, by the President's Strategic Defense Initiative. Whether or not the President's speech of March 1983 was premature, or even well advised, has now become a moot question. The President's "vision"—of a world delivered from the threat of nuclear annihilation through the marvels of American technology—touched off a controversy, marked by analyses and counter-analyses and much mutual recrimination, which will likely remain with us for many years.

The speech sparked a heated debate regarding the impact of strategic defense on American strategy, on the likely Soviet military response, on the arms competition, on U.S.-Soviet relations, and on our relations with our European allies. The irony is that this agitated discussion involved a research effort, whose fruits, if any, lie decades in the future. In the normal research program every effort is made to resolve the technical uncertainties prior to the time that conclusions are offered regarding strategy and force structure. Such regrettably has not been the case with the Strategic Defense Initiative, for all sorts of conclusions, some of them startling, are being offered regarding the impact of what still remains a research program on strategy and force structure decades hence.

Fears and hopes about Star Wars have come excessively to dominate the current policy scene. Internationally the United States is investing a very large share of its foreign policy capital in calming the apprehensions of its allies and in fending off attacks by the Soviets. Domestically discussion of defense policy has increasingly come to be dominated by the Star Wars debate even though the investigations into strategic defense technologies represent only a tiny fraction of our overall defense effort. For the foreseeable future, even in the eyes of supporters of the President's vision, the nation's security will rest on military programs and a force structure little influenced by strategic defense. Yet many important aspects of the nation's defense effort are now being neglected, at least comparatively, because of the intense focus on strategic defense.

An enduring national debate is ensured by the long-term nature of the SDI research effort and its immense potential impact both on arms competition and on U.S. relations with its allies and with the Soviet Union. That debate will be largely a *Congressional* debate. Ultimately the Star Wars issue is likely to be resolved by the Congress. After all, administrations come and go. After the initial controversy and the initial enthusiasm, the relevant research effort will extend over many years, longer than the life of any administration. Thus, it is more or less inevitable that the ultimate decisions regarding possible strategic defense deployments will be determined by the evolution of Congressional sentiment.

Senator Larry Pressler well understands that the long period of gestation for strategic defense technologies makes the Congressional debate the locus of ultimate decision. For this reason he has concentrated his own comprehensive investigation, which he once characterized as The Great Star Wars Debate, on the steadily unfolding debate of the Congress. It is a wise decision, for that debate is likely to have a far greater influence on the ultimate outcome than more technical studies. Senator Pressler has also, quite wisely, refrained from passing judgments. He presents the Congressional debates carefully, as they have evolved. He presents both the extreme views and the moderate views in the words of the participants—and leaves it to the reader to make his own assessment.

For the United States there is now no alternative to an extended and meticulous examination of the prospects for strategic defense. When a hope, so alluring to the public, that ballistic missiles may be effectively neutralized by American technology is held out by a President, there is no alternative in a democracy other than to explore the technical prospects—irrespective of the doubts of opponents. Moreover, the Soviet Union (despite the substantial measure of hypocrisy in its public position) has worked and continues vigorously to work on these technologies. The United States cannot responsibly avoid a major research effort in this area—simply to keep abreast of the Soviet Union.

Yet, even after the necessity for a major effort has been granted, certain questions remain to be resolved. There are three different potential focuses for the American effort—all of which are covered by the general rubric of Star Wars. The first is the pursuit of the President's vision of a strategic defense that can neutralize ballistic missiles, if not render nuclear weapons impotent and obsolete. The second is to concentrate on a far more limited and more near-term objective of protecting ballistic missile silos and other military targets. The third focus is even more constrained: to emphasize the research effort needed to reveal military options and to stay abreast of the Soviets—without any prior predilection regarding the desirability or nature of a hypothetical future deployment. Different individuals will vary in their selection of one of these three focuses. It should, however, be understood that the option of simply forgetting about strategic defense research is not seriously open to this country. It should also be noted that, irrespective of one's own preferences, it will be necessary to pursue the more visionary objective outlined by the President to the point of determining whether or not it is feasible, for that goal has now captured the public mind.

Within the Administration there has been considerable ambivalence regarding just where the emphasis should be placed. The President emphasizes a near-perfect defense that will make strategic offensive capabilities obsolescent. The Pentagon, by contrast, though it pays lip service to the President's vision as an ultimate goal, is concentrating on protection of our missile fields and other military targets as a way of strengthening deterrence. But there is a world of difference between the two. The President speaks of "protecting people—and not weapons," while the Pentagon pursues the precise opposite: "protecting weapons and not people." Needless to say the hold on the public imagination depends almost entirely on the former version. It is interesting to raise the question whether, if the public comes to believe there is no prospect of protecting our cities, there would still be sufficient willingness to undergo the heavy expenditures associated with protecting the missile fields.

Much enthusiasm has been generated about the prospects for strategic defense. In my judgment much of the enthusiasm is premature at best. Enthusiasm is fine in its place, but we must bear in mind that at this time the nation has only an array of technologies, some more distant, some closer at hand, under review. We are far, far away from being able to define a weapons system—particularly one that could achieve the rather grandiose objective of neutralizing the Soviet ballistic missile force.

It is the virtue of Larry Pressler's book that he brings all of us down to earth. By tracking the Congressional debate he examines the prospects for SDI technology, its implications for strategy, and the impact on alliance relations. The treatment reflects Senator Pressler's long-term interest and expertise in these matters. It should be recalled that two years prior to President Reagan's speech, Senator Pressler had already seen the implications of the technologies embodied in strategic defense for the vulnerability of our satellites—on which we depend for intelligence gathering and for command and control—and had introduced a Resolution (Senate Resolution 129) to limit the arms competition that has now been further accelerated by the revised emphasis on ballistic missile defense.

Pressler carefully develops the intimate connections between anti-satellite weapons and the technologies embodied in ballistic missile defense. He does so dispassionately, without pressing his own views on the reader. And he develops the overall questions involved in these new technologies in a context—that of Congressional debate—which is likely to prove decisive in determining which path this nation ultimately chooses.

James Schlesinger

Preface

Congress has been concerned for years about the placement of weapons in space by the superpowers. Hearings were held in Congress as early as 1979 to assess exotic space weapons technologies being developed by both the United States and the Soviet Union. It was not until March 23, 1983, however, that the general public became interested in this crucial issue. On that date President Ronald Reagan unveiled his Strategic Defense Initiative (SDI), popularly known as "Star Wars." In a televised speech, the president called on U.S. scientists to devise Antiballistic Missile (ABM) defenses that would render nuclear weapons "impotent and obsolete."

His speech riveted national and international attention on developing space weaponry and the increasing dangers of an arms race in space. But the concepts, issues, and esoteric, next-generation technologies that the SDI encompasses are difficult for most people to understand. As columnist William Safire has pointed out, even the program title, Strategic Defense Initiative, is difficult to remember because the initials do not form a catchy acronym. In his column in the *New York Times Magazine* of February 24, 1985, Safire invited his readers to coin a new term for the president's proposed global shield. He was inundated with responses, many of which he cited in a subsequent column on March 24, 1985. But the administration retained the term Strategic Defense Initiative, and the nickname Star Wars—which President Reagan distinctly dislikes—persisted.

The SDI is hard to comprehend for a more basic reason: It does not yet exist in the form of concrete weapons systems. It is a vision of possible new defense technologies, not a reality. What the president proposed was not the immediate deployment of a specific type of ABM system, but a research program designed to determine the technological feasibility of developing such a system—in the next decade or later.

Many people, however, believe the SDI commits the United States to deploy an ABM system once the technology is proven. Conflicting arguments have also been heard about the technological feasibility of the program, the costs involved, the impact on existing treaties, the reaction of the North Atlantic Treaty Organization allies, and even the program's ultimate goals. The SDI has created controversy on many fronts, resulting in media coverage that has sometimes given the public an inadequate understanding of the issue.

This book attempts to present an objective picture of the principal issues involved in the Star Wars debate with emphasis on congressional debate. It is a partial unfolding of a still-incomplete scenario. Years and probably decades of research, debate, and decision making lie ahead of us.

Congressional debate and basic studies used by Congress in these debates, principally between 1979 and 1985, are included here. Much has been written and said about the SDI debate in the media, and analysis abounds from journalists and scientists. However, no concise summary of the congressional debate and related official reports during these years has yet been written. This volume attempts to fill that void. It illustrates how difficult it is for Congress to dominate a controversial security issue such as the SDI. Congress has been asked to appropriate money for research —research that could have startling results but that encompasses objectives that are not yet very well defined.

The usual stages in the development of a new weapon include research, development, testing, evaluation, procurement, and deployment. Not every weapons proposal survives the scrutiny of the Pentagon or Congress through every stage, and the SDI will not be exempt from this careful development process.

The debate and related reports covered here illustrate that on weapons programs, Congress is inclined to justify support for large sums of research money well in advance of procurement decisions. For example, the B-1 bomber and MX missile programs, both important elements in U.S. defense modernization efforts, virtually became domestic jobs programs by the time Congress made a decision to procure these weapons systems. When research and development had been completed, these programs had acquired so much domestic constituent support it would have been almost impossible to reverse them, regardless of their actual worth to national defense. Many members of Congress justified voting for these systems as votes for continuing research until the point when prototypes had been built and large constituencies anticipated employment or other participation in their construction. It would appear the same thing could happen with the SDI, only more so because of the complexity of the problem and the potential size of procurement orders. The book illustrates that Congress has been struggling with great difficulty to more clearly define what it should do regarding the SDI, and will continue to do so.

The excerpts in this volume demonstrate how awkward it is for Congress to take leadership in this area, other than to potentially slow the program. By its nature, new weapons research must be conducted largely in secrecy, in a high-risk, highly classified environment. The executive branch has taken the initiative, and perhaps, as in the development of the atomic bomb, this is necessary. But in a democracy during peacetime, the SDI supporters in the administration have asked Congress to appropriate billions of dollars with very few concrete, specific expectations. The objective of an effective defense against nuclear missiles receives little opposition, and it is such a laudable goal that support for research in this area has been embraced by nearly every member of Congress, albeit at different levels.

For example, in Senate debate on June 4, 1985, Senator Bennett Johnston (D-La.), whose views are excerpted more fully in Chapter 7, pointed out that there is no evidence to support extravagant claims made about the SDI. "There has been no breakthrough. There has been no discovery. We are not on the threshold of building a new weapons system," Johnston said. "No, nothing has happened, except the President's speech. What did he say? The President said, 'We are going to build, in effect, an astrodome over the United States to make nuclear weapons obsolete'."[1]

Senator Sam Nunn (D-Ga.), while supporting increased funding of the SDI, agreed that Senator Johnston had a good point. "The Senator is correct, the program is ill defined by the administration. . . . We can certainly agree that the definition by the President is not something that can be taken seriously by people who have studied this. But the definition given by Paul Nitze is something different. The definition given by Secretary Weinberger is something different again. The definition given by General Abrahamson is something different again. So which definition are we going to choose?"[2]

Senator Malcolm Wallop (R-Wyo.) attacked this problem from another angle, offering an amendment to earmark $800 million for a system that could be deployed in five to seven years. "This amendment," Wallop stated, "proposes, strange to say, that we use a little of the money we spend to actually give something useful to ourselves."[3] Wallop's amendment would also have directed the secretary of defense to report to Congress a plan for the research and development program, addressing, among other things, the role that strategic defenses could play in enhancing the survivability and effectiveness of U.S. strategic forces. This amendment would have forced the administration to define the SDI in more practical terms. Wallop's amendment failed by a vote of 33 to 62.

In spite of many concerns over the direction and goals of the SDI program, the Senate finally approved $2.97 billion, and the House approved $2.5 billion, for research funding in fiscal year

1986, and at this writing the two houses seemed likely to compromise at the $2.75 billion level. The major reason for this support appeared to be the fact that arms control negotiations were taking place in Geneva. As Senator John Warner (R-Va.) said in response to an amendment that would have limited funding to $1.85 billion, "I would like the Senator to place himself in the seat of the U.S. negotiating team in Geneva when it hears that the Senate of the United States stripped out another billion dollars plus, from the program. . . . This would occur at the very time it seemed . . . this program . . . induced, more so than any other, the Soviets to return to the table; that it is this program which provides the key leverage."[4]

The 1985 congressional SDI debate, while approving a major funding increase for additional research, illustrates that questions and controversy continue. The argument that we must support our negotiators will cease to be convincing if some of the other concerns are not addressed adequately.

This book examines how we arrived at this point in the SDI debate. The early chapters present the antisatellite weapons debate in Congress. This debate was the precursor of the present SDI debate, which began with President Reagan's Star Wars speech of March 23, 1983. The remaining chapters review the SDI debate in both houses of Congress and the European perspective on the initiative. They also cover the details, perceptions, and analysis of space weaponry and arms control as presented to Congress in various reports.

In preparing this volume, searches were made of congressional hearing records, Senate and House floor statements, reports prepared for and considered by Congress, and reports prepared by and for the administration and Congress. Relevant transcripts from televised addresses and documentaries also were reviewed. Every effort was made to ensure that the viewpoints of both proponents and opponents were presented. The results provided here should help the reader form personal judgments on the promises and problems presented by the SDI.

This assembling of summaries from the principal reports considered by Congress and some of the congressional debate will furnish a source for the serious student who is interested in what Congress has considered. The bibliography provides a starting point for those who wish to know more about the congressional action, as well as other useful sources on the SDI. Many other fine speeches that have not been excerpted here have been given in both houses of Congress. These will be identified by the reader who investigates the debate further through the notes and the bibliography.

Contents

1

The Search for
A Perfect Defense

Let no one think that the expenditure of vast sums for systems and weapons of defense can guarantee absolute safety. The awful arithmetic of the atom bomb does not permit of any such easy solution.

The United States had unquestioned nuclear superiority when President Dwight D. Eisenhower made this statement in his Atoms for Peace speech at the United Nations on December 8, 1953. He warned that in the atomic age military strength does not guarantee security. "Even against the most powerful defense, an aggressor in possession of even the effective minimum number of atomic bombs for a surprise attack could probably place a sufficient number of his bombs on the chosen targets to cause hideous damage." President Eisenhower quickly added that the United States would take "swift and resolute" action in response to any such attack. The purpose of his speech, however, was not to emphasize U.S. power but to seek a solution to the arms race, which, in his words, "overshadows not only peace but the very life of the world."[1]

Thirty years after President Eisenhower delivered his warning about vast expenditures on weapons, President Ronald Reagan appeared on nationwide television to urge the nation's scientists to concentrate on research for a defensive shield against Soviet missiles. He explained that technological breakthroughs made such a defense possible.

If new technologies *do* produce a defense that cannot be countered, we will have written a new page in history; humans have searched throughout the ages for the ultimate weapon, the final word in defense. The Great Wall of China was to have deterred all

1

aggressors; the six-shooter was to have tamed the Wild West; the bomber was to have reduced any world war to a weekend-long affair; and multiple, independently targetable reentry vehicles (MIRVs) were to have provided the United States with a strategic advantage the Soviets could not match for many years. Always, however, the "perfect" weapon was matched, outclassed, or overcome with countermeasures. And newer weapons evolved, making the "ultimate" weapon of yesterday obsolete. As President Eisenhower's science advisor, R. Herbert York, once observed, "History has been littered with Maginot Lines."

Space weapons represent but the latest candidates in the human search for the perfect defense. They quietly emerged in the 30-year interim between Eisenhower's Atoms for Peace speech and President Reagan's Strategic Defense Initiative (SDI) address. President Eisenhower's advice was not followed, however, even in the time before new scientific research offered the promise of effective space defenses. During these three decades, the U.S. defensive strategies ranged from the crash buildup started by President John F. Kennedy to the measured standoff represented by the concept of mutually assured destruction (MAD), with its reliance on offensive weapons and the threat of retaliation.

John F. Kennedy campaigned for office in 1960 warning that the Soviets had pulled ahead of the United States in nuclear strength and calling for a defense buildup. In 1961, however, satellite photographs of Soviet missiles and bomber facilities revealed that the missile gap, which had played such a prominent role in Kennedy's campaign, was in favor of the United States instead of the Soviet Union. U.S. nuclear superiority was still clearly established at the time of the 1962 Cuban missile crisis, precipitated when Premier Nikita Khrushchev stationed Soviet intermediate-range missiles on the U.S. southern flank in Cuba. President Kennedy marshaled considerable air and naval strength and brought the full weight of U.S. diplomacy to bear. As Secretary of State Dean Rusk put it, the Russians "blinked" and removed their missiles.

The Cuban crisis spurred both the United States and the Soviet Union to increase the technological sophistication of their nuclear arsenals. The next decade witnessed a prime example of what arms control experts call the action–reaction cycle. The Soviets gained parity with the United States. Both sides began developing Antiballistic Missiles (ABMs) with limited capabilities to intercept Intercontinental Ballistic Missiles (ICBMs). In 1967, the emergence of a potential ballistic missile defense (BMD) by the Soviet Union led Defense Secretary Robert McNamara to authorize the testing of

MIRVs. The United States subsequently deployed MIRVs on Minuteman III and Poseidon missiles. This revolutionized weapons technology. MIRVs enable one missile to carry up to ten or more warheads, each aimed at a different target. At a certain point, the warheads separate from their launching missile, greatly increasing the destructive potential of a single missile. By 1971, the Soviets had deployed their own ICBMs with multiple reentry vehicles. Today, many U.S. officials believe that MIRVs deployed by the Soviets leave U.S. Minuteman and Peacekeeper (MX) missiles vulnerable.

Other arms control experts now look on the failure to limit MIRV launchers in the 1972 Strategic Arms Limitation Talks (SALT) I treaty as one of the most disappointing results of the arms control process. Henry Kissinger told reporters in 1974, "I would say in retrospect that I wish I had thought through the implications of a MIRVed world more thoughtfully than I did in 1969 and 1970."[2]

The United States was developing its own primitive BMD as early as the 1950s, when the army first began testing the Nike–Zeus system. Both Presidents Eisenhower and Kennedy opposed funding for the system because of limited confidence in its capability. The system's successor, the Nike X, was considered technically superior, but it, too, had problems. President Lyndon B. Johnson ultimately scrapped plans to install either system.

The Soviets, however, installed their ABM system, the Galosh, around Moscow between 1966 and 1968. They have continued modernization of the Moscow system since that time. Both the United States and the Soviet Union designed their earliest ABM systems to protect people. Both sides ultimately acknowledged that their systems would have limited effectiveness against a massive nuclear strike, and would provide protection only against attack from a second-rank nuclear power.

At the 1967 U.S.–Soviet summit, held in Glassboro, New Jersey, President Johnson proposed arms control negotiations between the superpowers. The Soviets agreed, but no date for the meeting was set. President Johnson, meanwhile, was committed to production of another missile defense system, the Sentinel. Defense Secretary McNamara described the system as both "marginal" and designed to provide only limited defense of several major cities. Even this limited plan triggered strong protests from citizens who did not relish the idea of nuclear-tipped ABM systems in their backyards. The outcry led newly elected President Richard M. Nixon to suspend the Sentinel program. In announcing his decision, Nixon said, "Although every instinct motivates me to provide the American people with complete protection against a major nuclear attack, it is not within our power to do so. The heaviest defense system we con-sidered—one designed to protect our major cities—still could not prevent a catastrophic level of U.S. fatalities from a deliberate all-out Soviet attack."[3]

In March 1969, President Nixon announced plans for a more sophisticated ABM system, the Safeguard. It emphasized defense of missile sites instead of defense of cities. This also met with heated opposition, but the Senate finally approved funding for Safeguard in August 1969—by a one-vote margin. Construction of a Safeguard site began at the Grand Forks, North Dakota, Air Force Base missile field in 1970.

A few months earlier, in 1969, the Soviet Union and the United States had opened SALT negotiations. A major factor in bringing both sides to the negotiating table was the recognition that ABM systems were marginally effective, extremely expensive to con-struct and operate, and likely to accelerate the arms race.

After two and one-half years of negotiation, SALT I concluded with the signing of two documents. The first, known as the Interim Agreement, established temporary limits on the number of U.S. and Soviet offensive ballistic missile launchers. The second, known as the Antiballistic Missile Treaty, placed permanent limits on the deployment of ABM systems in the United States and the Soviet Union. A Democrat-controlled Senate consented in August 1972 to the ratification of an ABM treaty negotiated with the Soviet Union by a Republican administration.

With the signing of the ABM treaty and the deployment of MIRVs by both sides came the new strategic situation referred to earlier—MAD, or mutually assured destruction. In short, the nuclear deterrence theory held that neither superpower would engage in nuclear war with the other. The risks were too high. Even if one power launched a surprise attack, the other would have suffi-cient retaliatory forces to destroy the attacking nation. Destruction therefore was mutually assured, and a balance of terror came into being.

This strategy, the dominant one today, has its drawbacks. One such flaw centers on the risk of nuclear war caused by accident or misunderstanding. The proposed solution to this grim possibility rests upon arms control agreements that would reduce the number of nuclear weapons and missiles. Attempts at such agreements have foundered. A related effort would also improve communications between Washington and Moscow to lessen the chance of accident. The improved hot-line communications between the two capitals is an example.

Another flaw in the theory is that it says little or nothing about nonnuclear wars. The U.S. solution was twofold: to maintain sufficient conventional forces in Europe to discourage Soviet adventurism while concurrently negotiating for mutual reductions of conventional forces. Ultimately, though, U.S. strategy depends upon the use of tactical nuclear weapons to defend against a Soviet attack in Europe. Supporters of the doctrine of massive retaliation assume that the danger of an escalation to strategic nuclear weapons will likewise preclude the outbreak of hostilities in Europe. In addition to maintaining minimally sufficient conventional forces, the United States has also participated in arms control talks that would reduce or stabilize forces in Central Europe and implement measures to reduce the risk of war. The Mutual and Balanced Force Reduction Talks, begun in 1973 between the Warsaw Pact and and most North Atlantic Treaty Organization (NATO) nations, have dragged on for over a decade without an agreement on a reduction in forces. The 1975 Helsinki Accords implemented some confidence-building measures designed to reduce the outbreak of war due to misunderstandings. One such measure provides for observers from the West at military exercises of the Warsaw Pact countries and vice versa. The assumption is that such observers can provide assurances that the exercise is not a guise for a surprise attack. The Conference on Security and Cooperation in Europe with its 35 participants and its offspring, the Conference on Disarmament in Europe, continue to pursue these objectives, but the pace is glacial.

The third and perhaps most serious chink in the armor of the massive retaliation strategy results from changes in technology. Satellite communications have become increasingly important to all major nations. For the United States and the Soviet Union, they have become critical as the eyes and, to an extent, the ears of the intelligence-gathering system. Without satellite reconnaissance, there would have been no SALT I agreement. Neither side would have been able to verify the missile activity and deployment status of the other. The existence and importance of these and other military satellites, however, invited the development of antisatellite (ASAT) weapons. Some of the research for such weapons, as well as for new or improved BMD weapons, ironically, has been sanctioned, or even encouraged, by the ABM treaty itself. The treaty contains no limitations on laboratory research. They were not included in part as a hedge against one side breaking the accord and in part because no system was (or is) capable of verifying laboratory research activity.

It is this last drawback—the new technologies—that provides the greatest threat to the survival of massive retaliation as the fundamental war deterrence strategy. Shortly after President Reagan's startling speech on March 23, 1983, Dr. Edward Teller, a leading nuclear physicist and proponent of the SDI, explained to the House Armed Services Committee how his own thinking about the national defense situation has changed over the decades. "At the end of the First World War it was clear that defense is stronger than offense. . . . In the Second World War, this doctrine was overturned. We developed the atomic bomb. We had a weapon which could not be beaten, against which there could never be a defense."[4]

Now the situation is changing again, Dr. Teller said, because of new weapons that can be used "not for mass destruction, but to destroy very specific targets such as offensive weapons in action,"

"In the 1950s, I taught no defense," he continued. "In the 1960s, I was doubtful. In the 1970s, I was hopeful about defense. And now I know it's feasible because I have seen at least half a dozen solid defense proposals.

"The President's [SDI] proposal is based on foresight rather than hindsight. It is based on the extensive human experience that whatever fantastic weapons of destruction have been constructed may be countered by the ingenuity of every progressing technology and science.

"It is, of course, admitted that the use of defense for deterrence and thereby for the avoidance of war will be an extremely difficult job. Fortunately, our young scientists have come forward with a number of truly ingenious ideas utilizing the remarkable energy concentrations that can be created in atomic bombs or in lasers which generate light beams, more generally electromagnetic beams that can be of extreme intensity and remarkably well-defined directionality. These are two striking examples, but they don't begin to exhaust the list of candidates for defensive weapons. . . .

There are at least half a dozen basically different approaches to strategic defense, some employing lasers and others not. I consider it a virtual certainty that some of them will work, and will shift the balance of forces back in favor of defense."

It is this challenge to the nuclear war deterrence strategy that Congress and the nation must consider. The remainder of this book discusses the two vital applications of the new technologies affecting defense. The first of these is ASAT weapons, an exceedingly important subject in its own right and one that the SDI has tended to overshadow. It should be remembered, however, that even were the SDI to be abandoned as impracticable by the current or a future administration, the question of ASAT weapons would remain. The second is the impact of the SDI—its technology, costs, and strategic implications.

2

Congress Reviews
The Antisatellite Program

Although Congress had addressed the issue of weapons in space during its deliberations over the Outer Space Treaty in the 1960s and the ABM treaty in the early 1970s, interest waned thereafter. Yet, throughout the 1960s and 1970s, both superpowers carried out research and testing of ASAT and other space weapons. The Soviets tested their ground-based, explosive-type ASAT 16 times between 1968 and 1978. This ASAT uses a variant of the older model SS-9/Scarp missile to launch an interceptor into orbit. The interceptor can then maneuver near its target and destroy it. Although there is evidence that the Soviets have conducted research on direct-ascent missiles with nuclear warheads, lasers, and space-based systems, only the orbital interceptor is considered operational.

For its part, the United States, after abandoning its ground-based ASAT system in the mid-1970s, concentrated upon development of an air-launched system. The present concept, which has undergone limited testing, uses an F-15 aircraft to carry a two-stage rocket high into the atmosphere, where it is then released. The rocket launches a miniature homing vehicle that is capable of tracking and destroying a target in space. The United States also has an active program for developing technology for both space- and ground-based laser weapons that could have ASAT applications.

The Carter administration, motivated in large part by concern for the progress of the Soviet ASAT effort, initiated negotiations in 1978. Congress and the public paid little attention. Three rounds were held before the talks lapsed following the Soviet invasion of Afghanistan in late 1979. With the Afghanistan situation, the Iranian hostage crisis, and the U.S. Olympic boycott getting the headlines, the disruption of the ASAT talks seemed to be but one more sign of deteriorating relations with the Soviets. The Reagan administration made no attempt to resume the ASAT talks.[1]

The launching in April 1981 of the first reusable spacecraft, the Columbia space shuttle, rekindled congressional interest in the ASAT talks. Scientists optimistically proclaimed that the advent of the shuttle placed the world on the threshold of a new era in the scientific and commercial development of space. This technology could promote revolutions in communications, meteorology, navigation, resource exploration, and scientific discovery. For the first time it would be possible to perform numerous repair missions on satellites, conduct unique research in science and manufacturing, and make multiple trips at a fraction of the cost of launching and preparing a new space vehicle for each space voyage.

But the advent of the space shuttle had its dark side. The Soviets, obviously alarmed by the success of the mission, denounced the space shuttle as a weapons system, and introduced a treaty in the United Nations that called for a ban on the use of the shuttle for military purposes. From the point of view of the United States, there was also a dark side. The shuttle would be highly vulnerable to Soviet ASAT weapons, as it was virtually indefensible in space.[2]

The development of Soviet and U.S. ASAT programs and the launch of the space shuttle all seemed to presage an arms race in space. It was in response to this ominous situation that the Pressler resolution (S.Res. 129) was first introduced on May 6, 1981. The remainder of this chapter recounts the journey of that resolution and related legislative action up to the summer of 1984, when both the Senate and the House held major debates on the ASAT program.

The May 6, 1981, introduction of S.Res. 129 was a key step in an effort to bring the issue to the public's attention. It seemed obvious that the safer, less costly, and more logical approach to the problem was first to try to avert the space arms race through negotiations for a verifiable ban on space weapons. Yet neither side was making any movement in this direction. There were other potential problems with a space arms race. A BMD might be developed, threatening the ABM treaty and costing enormous amounts of money. With the United States more dependent on satellites than the Soviets, the United States had the most to lose in a space arms race. The statement introducing the resolution included the following remarks by Senator Pressler. "I rise today to offer a resolution expressing the sense of the Senate with respect to resuming negotiations with the Soviet Union on the limitation of antisatellite (ASAT) weapons systems.

"In view of the extraordinary prospects for the peaceful use of space now before us, it is with special concern and alarm that I call the Senate's attention to another, singularly ominous development related to mankind's use of space: The development by the Soviet Union and the United States of sophisticated weapons systems designed exclusively to intercept, damage or destroy orbiting satellites. . . .

"The Soviet 'killer satellite' program has been widely covered in the press, and as former Secretary of Defense Harold Brown revealed in 1977, it has been operational for a number of years. As recently as March of this year, the Soviets conducted yet another test in space of their ASAT weapon, this time using a new, improved homing device to close on, and then destroy a target satellite. . . .

"I am not particularly interested at this point in getting mired down in a debate over which side started this particular arms race. What I am concerned about is the complete lack of movement toward negotiating realistic limitations on the development and use of this type of weaponry. . . . Given the current level of R&D [research and development] effort by both sides, the day when new ASAT weapons are operational is not very distant.

"My mystification over the lack of movement on this issue is compounded by the realization that both the United States and the Soviet Union have repeatedly recorded and endorsed the principle of the peaceful utilization of space. In the preamble to the Outer Space Treaty, both nations formally recognized the common interest of all mankind in the progress of the exploration and use of outer space for peaceful purposes. . . .

"As a first step in halting a very costly and counterproductive race in ASAT weaponry, I propose that new ASAT negotiations focus on the following objectives. First, a comprehensive ban on the actual use of ASAT weapons. Second, a moratorium, whose duration can be later determined, on further testing in space of any weapons systems designed exclusively to intercept, damage or destroy orbiting satellites. Third, the dismantling and destruction of the Soviet 'killer satellite' system now operational. Last, stringent verification measures covering each party's compliance with each of the above provisions. . . . Any agreement limiting ASAT weaponry should not interfere with legitimate R&D activities permitted under the ABM Treaty."[3]

The first congressional hearing on space arms control was held on September 2, 1982, before the Senate Foreign Relations Arms Control Subcommittee. The subcommittee examined the background of space arms talks and potential Soviet capabilities.

Still, there was not enough congressional support to take action on the resolution before Congress adjourned in 1982.

When the Ninety-Eighth Congress convened, a revised Pressler resolution (S.Res. 43) was offered. This resolution reflected a heightened awareness that ASATs were only part of the problem. Other space-based and space-directed weapons, such as BMDs, needed a higher priority on the space arms control agenda.

The reasons for revising S.Res. 129 were explained in the statement by Senator Pressler introducing S.Res. 43 on February 2, 1983. "Let us remember that in these and in other ways the military has a vital role to play in space. For instance, the missile gap of the late 1950s ended only after our first reconnaissance satellites provided a clearer picture of the Soviet missile force. The hostage rescue attempt of two years ago would have been nearly impossible without direct satellite links.

"Were it not for space systems, arms control agreements might be impossible to achieve. Let me note that even if we manage to improve arms control verification through onsite inspection, space systems will remain a vital element in assuring compliance with treaties. Inspectors on the ground will need space systems to identify events and locations that require inspection.

"After a quarter-century of serving the common good through the exploration and utilization of space, we are now at an ominous crossroads. . . . The U.S. ASAT is approaching the testing phase. Once testing and deployment occurs, it will be increasingly difficult to produce a verifiable ban on ASATs and on space weapons in general."[4]

The rationale behind expanding the resolution to deal with outer space weapons in general rather than just ASATs in particular was therefore simple: Outer space played an important part in arms control verification. With space weapons deployed, verification would be impossible and verification tools would be easily vulnerable. That could endanger the entire arms control process if allowed to continue.

The Tsongas resolution (S.J.Res. 28), introduced the next day, was slightly different. This resolution called for the United States to begin negotiations with the Soviets for a complete ban on space weaponry. It also called for a U.N. effort to extend the 1967 Outer Space Treaty to include a ban on all weapons based in space for use against any target, and a ban on all ASATs regardless of where they are based. Congressman John Joseph Moakley (D-Mass.) previously had introduced an identical resolution in the House of Representatives.

In his statements introducing the Tsongas–Moakley resolution, Senator Paul Tsongas (D-Mass.) explained the dangers of a space arms race: "Sometime this year the Air Force is expected to test an antisatellite weapon (ASAT) to be launched from a high-flying F-15 fighter aircraft. . . . The U.S. ASAT will greatly outperform the Soviet counterpart, although it too can reach only satellites in low-Earth orbit.

"Once our system is tested, every F-15 becomes a potential ASAT platform, making a verifiable ban on ASAT weapons virtually impossible. Without a treaty prohibiting further ASAT development, we can expect the Soviets to match us system for system and dollar for dollar. . . .

"Already under way is the next, still more costly, step in the space war: Weapons to destroy ballistic missiles, including Star Wars style laser and particle beam weapons. Such systems are not just science fiction; they are now being developed, both in this country and the Soviet Union, for deployment before the end of the century."[5]

Senator Tsongas also reiterated the danger to weather, reconnaissance, treaty verification, and early warning satellite systems. Explaining the dangers involved and efforts that would be necessary to undertake a space weapons race, he asked in conclusion, "Do we want to pay for these systems? Or, on the contrary, do we want a peaceful space where civilian enterprises can operate free of war and weapons?"

The effort to extend arms control to outer space weapons went beyond the attempts at passing Senate resolutions. In January and February 1983, before the president's SDI speech, the Senate considered the nomination of Kenneth L. Adelman for the directorship of the Arms Control and Disarmament Agency (ACDA). Some on the Foreign Relations Committee were skeptical about the choice of Adelman for this position. One of the reasons for skepticism was his views on space arms control. It is important to note, however, that the views Adelman presented to the committee were generally the same as the official administration position. Adelman's testimony demonstrated the basic administration view on space arms control at that time.

Senator Pressler. My question is, Should we not negotiate [ASATs] directly with the Soviets now?

Mr. Adelman. We are negotiating, in a sense, in the 40-member Committee on Disarmament, and we are discussing space issues. The Soviets are present in these meetings.

Senator Pressler. Why that Committee— . . . only the Soviets and the United States have ASAT weapons?

Mr. Adelman. Senator Pressler, the United States does not have ASAT capability right now. If your question is whether a bilateral approach is better than a multilateral approach, that would depend on the progress made in the multilateral approach and whether we should continue on the pattern that was successful with regard to the Outer Space Treaty where issues were addressed and put in a multilateral treaty. . . .

Senator Pressler. You have said that verification is a major source of delaying ASAT talks. Do you believe as I do that once we test and deploy our ASAT system, verification will be an even more difficult problem?

Mr. Adelman. I think the problems in verification . . . are very extensive. There are very few systems; they are systems that can be enacted relatively—with many deceptive devices, et cetera.[6]

From the testimony of Mr. Adelman, it became clear that the administration was in no hurry to resume ASAT arms control talks. Its rationale was twofold. First, it said that the 40-nation Committee on Disarmament meeting in Geneva was the proper forum for ASAT talks. The administration apparently wanted to use the existence of those talks as a basis for avoiding bilateral negotiations. Second, the administration claimed that no ASAT limitation was verifiable. Senate hearings on ASAT verification showed that although the administration did have a valid point on some counts, some ASAT limits were theoretically verifiable. The Pressler and Tsongas resolutions did not tie the hands of the administration if ASATs were ultimately unverifiable; they sought only to set in motion negotiations to explore the possibilities for verification.

On March 23, 1983, President Reagan gave his speech establishing the SDI. From that point on, the efforts of the Senate on this issue moved from the position of little or no public interest to the forefront of close public scrutiny.

Additional hearings were held on April 14 and May 18, 1983. During the hearings, testimony was delivered by a panel organized by the Union of Concerned Scientists. Dr. Kurt Gottfried testified as the director of the organization. A professor of physics and nuclear studies at Cornell University, Gottfried stressed that it was imperative to stop immediately the growth of Soviet ASAT capabilities. Noting that the Soviet draft treaty on ASATs did not prohibit the testing of ground-based ASATs in space, Gottfried offered what his group believed would be the best agreement. "No weapon that can destroy, damage, render inoperable, or change the flight trajectory of space objects can be tested in space or against space objects.

"We have compared the status and potential capabilities of both systems and conclude that an immediate moratorium on ASAT space tests would not jeopardize our security if negotiations were to fail, or if a treaty were eventually abrogated or circumvented by the Soviet Union," Gottfried testified.

"In conclusion, I want to make the point that Senator Pressler made earlier, the remarkable parallel between the history of MIRV and the development of ASAT that we can see in front of us. The Soviets failed to foresee that we would develop MIRVs as a sophisticated response to their primitive missile defense of Moscow.

"We, in turn, did not anticipate that our response would eventually boomerang by putting all our silo-based missiles at risk. Today, there is general agreement that we would have been far better off had we abstained from introducing MIRVs. This lesson applies directly to anti-satellite weapons.

"The Soviets have been both foolish and reckless to spend some 15 years nurturing a clumsy threat against a rather small portion of our satellites. Their major accomplishment has been to provoke us into building a far more sophisticated system.

"But, as with ballistic missiles, an ongoing competition in space weaponry will, inexorably, reduce the security of both sides. That should be clear to everyone by now, I would hope. Or, do we have to wait for a presidential commission to tell us a decade from now that in 1983 the United States blundered yet again by upping the ante in the deadly poker game of nuclear war?"[7]

On July 14, 1983, S.J.Res. 129 was introduced in the Senate by Senators Pressler, Tsongas, Percy, Pell, Mathias, and Cranston. That resolution was the product of hearings and compromises on S.Res. 129 from the Ninety-Seventh Congress, S.Res. 43 and S.J.Res. 28 from the current Ninety-Eighth Congress, as well as information about parallel actions in the House of Representatives. Senator Tsongas summed up the mood of the resolution's authors: "Today I join Senator Pressler in introducing a joint resolution calling upon the President to negotiate an end to the arms race in space. The Administration has failed to negotiate—or even attempt to negotiate—a halt in the development of antisatellite weapons by the Soviet Union. Unless such development is stopped, the day is imminent when our most important and sensitive military satellites will be in jeopardy."[8]

Noting Soviet Premier Yuri Andropov's statement that the arms race would spill over into space without a treaty, Tsongas asserted that both sides knew what was at stake and that there was no excuse not to negotiate. Quoting from a report on space weapons prepared by the Union of Concerned Scientists, Tsongas reiterated that satellites were more important to U.S. than Soviet defense. Because the present Soviet ASAT was not able to strike most U.S. satellites, a verifiable agreement could still be reached, he claimed.

Senator Claiborne Pell (D-R.I.) also spoke on behalf of the resolution, stating that the three Foreign Relations Committee hearings on the subject had convinced him that "we should give high national priority to efforts to deal with antisatellite weapons and weapons in space."[9]

On July 18, 1983, Senator Tsongas offered a variation of this resolution as an amendment (No. 1518) to the 1984 Omnibus Defense Authorization Bill (S. 675). The amendment required the president, before testing the U.S. F-15 ASAT, to certify that the United States was endeavoring in good faith to negotiate a ban on ASAT weapons and that failure to conduct an ASAT test would pose clear and irrevocable harm to the national security.

In his opening statement, Senator Tsongas described to the Senate much of what happened in the Foreign Relations Committee hearings and reviewed what had been said already on the floor regarding S.J.Res. 129. Calling the Soviet ASAT a "bulky and cumbersome weapon," Tsongas explained that now was the time to negotiate. "If we proceed with testing of antisatellite weapons, we stand to lose forever the chance we have of negotiating an end to the arms race in space."[10]

Before many senators would support the amendment, however, they wanted to know exactly what "endeavoring to negotiate in good faith" meant. The following exchange between Senators Tsongas and John Warner (R-Va.) made clear the meaning of that phrase:

Senator Warner. It is my understanding that during the course of our discussions, the principal sponsor of the amendment . . . has agreed that the intent of this language is not to require before such certification is in order that the United States be actually engaged in bilateral negotiations with the Soviet Union on an antisatellite weapon ban. Is that understanding accurate?

Senator Tsongas. The Senator is correct. . . . Obviously, it would be my preference to have actual bilateral negotiations on the subject under way already. It is my belief, however, that in recognition of the many complex and difficult issues that are involved, a certification that a serious examination of the issues relevant to a verifiable antisatellite weapons ban was under way, coupled with a certification of willingness on the part of the U.S. Government to negotiate such a ban, would indeed suffice for the purpose of satisfying the requirements of this amendment.

Senator Warner. In view of that, I wish to advise the distinguished Senator from Massachusetts that with that clarification of the modification incorporated in the amendment, namely those concerning explosive or inert antisatellite warhead flight testing against space objects, the managers of the bill are prepared to accept the amendment.[11]

Acceptance of the amendment by the managers of the bill for the Armed Services Committee paved the way for unanimous passage by a vote of 91 to 0.

Most administration officials were under the impression that the amendment had no real effect on U.S. policy. After all, how could anyone clearly define "good faith" endeavors or a "clear and irrevocable harm to national security"? It was only after it became apparent that the amendment actually limited executive action that the administration defined all ASAT limits as unverifiable, making negotiations for a verifiable treaty impossible. The administration did this in the hope that the amendment would fail if it were reintroduced. Since the amendment had been tied to the defense authorization bill, it was valid for only one year.

Following passage of the Tsongas amendment, supporters of S.J.Res. 129 persisted in their efforts to get the resolution passed into law. If it were adopted separately on its own merits, rather than being incorporated into the defense authorization bill, it would not be subject to the one-year expiration date. Further hearings were held in the Foreign Relations Committee on this resolution, and another report was released by the committee in November 1983.

Another hearing was held on April 25, 1984, in which testimony on the findings of the president's strategic defense studies was received from administration witnesses, including Lt. General James Abrahamson, the newly designated director of the SDI office in the Pentagon. The Office of Technology Assessment (OTA)—the congressional research arm on technological issues—also delivered its preliminary assessment of strategic defense. ACDA Director Kenneth Adelman explained administration policy at the hearing, and additional views were presented by a panel of outside experts. The administration's position was also articulated in a report requested by Congress in late 1983 and released on March 31, 1984.

The purpose of the April 25, 1984, hearing was to consider the immediate concerns raised by ASAT weapons and long-term implications of futuristic strategic defenses, particularly the administration plan to spend $26 billion on a five-year research effort. This expenditure represented only the down payment on a system requiring $500 billion to $1 trillion or more if deployed. The hearing affirmed that many Defense Department specialists were skeptical of the feasibility of a total defense. They increasingly drew attention to technological hurdles to be overcome before advanced missile defenses would be possible. At the same time, less was being said about people protection. Protection of missile silos against nuclear attack had begun to replace civilian defense as the justification for developing beam weaponry.

Immediately after the April hearing, efforts to bring the resolution to a vote by the full Senate intensified. New Senate cosponsors were added, and Congressman Norman Dicks (D-Wash.), joined by Les Aspin (D-Wisc.) and Albert Gore (D-Tenn.), introduced the resolution in the House of Representatives and brought it before the House Foreign Affairs Committee.

To broaden the list of Senate supporters, S.J.Res. 129 was modified by an amendment introduced by Senator Charles H. Percy (R-Ill.) for Senator Pressler, himself, and 31 others, on May 23:

Senator Percy. What this amendment says is that the Senate simply does not agree with the Administration's decision not to enter into any negotiations on space-based or space-directed weaponry. We believe the United States should propose such negotiations, if not on a total ban, then at least on as strict a set of restrictions as can be negotiated. . . .

The amendment also underscores our belief that arms control should precede any decision to deploy elements of the SDI. We do not believe that arms control in space should be held in abeyance for years while development of SDI programs carries forward, as the President's science adviser recommended in testimony before the Foreign Relations Committee on April 25. If we were to accept this approach, we would only ensure that development of space-based weaponry would proceed beyond the point where arms control could ever be expected to save us from an unregulated competition.

Senator Pressler. We are of the view that an agreement controlling space weapons can be achieved, given seriousness and flexibility on both sides in negotiations. Claims that any and all types of space weapons agreements cannot be verified are without foundation. Many leading experts have stated that many space arms control arrangements can be effectively verified. This view is shared by a panel of specialists convened at my request by the Office of Technology Assessment. . . .

This amendment reinforces our commitment to strong and effective verification procedures by calling for increased funding to enhance U.S. monitoring and verification capabilities.

In cases where an outright ban on ASAT weapons is blocked for lack of sufficient verification capabilities, this amendment urges that "strict limitations" be imposed instead. . . .

As for other systems with significant ASAT potential, the United States should seek strict limitations in an ASAT accord. . . .

This amendment aims to improve upon Senate Joint Resolution 129. We believe that this new language clarifies our position on the need for talks with the Soviet Union.[12]

Senator Patrick J. Leahy (D-Vt.), a member of the Senate Intelligence Committee, also expressed his support for the amended resolution, saying, "It is difficult to conceive of anything more dangerous or destabilizing during an intensive crisis between the United States and the Soviet Union than real or perceived acts aimed at each other's warning and reconnaissance satellites." Leahy also expressed concerns about ASATs becoming a backdoor circumvention of the ABM treaty.[13]

Despite strong support for the amended Pressler–Tsongas resolution, opponents of the measure successfully opposed debating it on the Senate floor. Instead, the resolution was debated as an amendment to the defense authorization bill on June 12, 1984. That debate is the subject of Chapter 5.

The Senate floor debate marked an inconclusive culmination of three years of hearings, compromises, testimony from experts, studies of the problem, and alternative legislative proposals. It illustrates the slowness or deliberateness with which the Senate, and Congress, approach consideration of significant public policy issues. When the Senate is not ready to make a decision, it defers final action and, in the process, encourages further debate and the development of compromise legislation. Nevertheless, the space weapons debate in Congress had begun, and the accumulated efforts of the 1981–84 period would continue to influence future decisions by Congress on this issue. The debate on the ASAT resolutions and amendments would provide useful information for the more encompassing SDI debates of 1984–85 and beyond.

The F-15 ASAT is the least dramatic element of any future space weapons race. Without arms restraints, more costly ASAT deployments will surely follow. After the U.S. ASAT becomes operational, the Soviets may decide that their current ASAT is no longer enough. U.S. defense planners in turn will begin to experiment on countermeasures to the newer system, and still more advanced ASAT systems and satellite protective countermeasures will be studied.

Looking beyond the F-15-based ASAT, press reports suggest the possible future direction of this weapon technology. According to *Aviation Week*, Air Force Space Command wishes to develop a laser ASAT system to complement (if not replace) the F-15 ASAT—not because it believes the F-15 weapon will not work, but because of an expanded list of potential ASAT targets that have evolved since the

F-15 system was conceived. Still other ASAT concepts have been examined and potentially could be developed.

Once the path toward space weapons deployments is joined, the space arms race may develop a momentum of its own. Eventually, whether it is planned or not, the United States may find itself buying ASATs to match Soviet ASATs, and defensive satellites to act as guardians against a growing Soviet ASAT potential. Defensive satellites could be accompanied by expensive satellite-hardening techniques and other passive countermeasures. A Department of Defense study presented to the Senate Armed Services Committee estimated that a laser defensive satellite capability would cost as much as an offensive ASAT capability.

Given defensive satellites and other countermeasures, ASATs would have to be adapted to their more complex attack mission. Overwhelming hardening techniques would require increased laser power. Contending with maneuverable systems would require a more effective method for command, control, tracking, and damage assessment. Lasers would become progressively more powerful and the sensors for detecting and responding to targets more sensitive. Computer requirements and capabilities would increase accordingly. Eventually, whether it was planned or not, an ASAT could have all the capabilities for a limited attack on ICBMs. Further along in the development of technology, these primitive BMDs could become increasingly capable of attacking a larger number of missiles and nuclear warheads. Thus, in the natural course of ASAT modernization, the United States could move from the simple F-15-launched ASAT to a complex, SDI-type anti-ICBM weapons system.

This is a vitally important consideration. Deployment of ASATs could be a monumental step toward strategic defense deployments.

3

Congressional Antisatellite Hearings and Reports

During the course of the last chapter, there were repeated references to congressional hearings on ASATs. Hearings are a primary means by which the Senate and House gather information on various issues. In the case of ASATs, congressional committees and subcommittees held seven hearings between September 1982 and June 1984. Five of these occurred prior to the full-fledged ASAT debates in the House in May 1984 and in the Senate the following month. A close reading of those debates reveals that many speakers drew heavily upon the testimony presented in the hearings.

Other congressional sources of information included a report on ASATs prepared by the Senate Foreign Relations Committee in November 1983; comments of a panel of experts on ASATs brought together by OTA, an arm of Congress; and a report from the administration requested by Congress in the fall of 1983 and presented on March 31, 1984. Two hearings regarding the administration report took place in June 1984 following the major debates on ASATs, but the report itself and various commentaries on it were available prior to the debates.

This chapter includes excerpts from these hearings, the OTA panel, and the reports, as well as one speech given on the floor of the Senate. The arrangement is topical rather than chronological. After a review of the 1978–79 negotiations, three key issues of ASATs and space weaponry are highlighted: (1) Soviet attitudes toward space arms talks, (2) U.S. ASAT testing, and (3) the relationship between ASAT and BMD technology. The last part discusses the administration's ASAT report to Congress with particular emphasis on its contention that an ASAT agreement is not verifiable.

One of the most eloquent testimonials on the subject of ASATs came from former Secretary of State Dean Rusk, who wrote the following in 1983 to the Senate Foreign Relations Arms Control Subcommittee: "When we look down the road to the possibility of the movement of active weapons into outer space, I find the prospect very foreboding. We must assume that the Soviets would be able to do whatever we can do in outer space and that there is no possibility of gaining any unilateral national advantage. More importantly, however, if one or both sides begin to approach feasible space weapons such as lasers or particle beams, we can be certain that there would be a frantic race on both sides to devise offensive weapons which could penetrate or evade such defenses. . . .

"It seems almost insane to go down this road without a major effort to prevent an outer space arms race. . . .

"I should also like to see my grandchildren look up into the vast universe and reflect with the psalmist that the heavens declare the glory of God—and not the folly of man."[1]

Negotiators from the United States and the Soviet Union held three rounds of talks in 1978–79 on a possible ASAT treaty. The talks were broken off by the United States after the Soviet invasion of Afghanistan.

During a Foreign Relations Committee hearing on September 20, 1982, Robert W. Buchheim, who headed the U.S. delegation to the negotiations, was asked why the talks were abandoned.

Mr. Buchheim. . . . In the summer of 1979 . . . the two delegations . . . had clearly come to a point where they both acknowledged, as they had at the end of the preceding two rounds, that about as much progress had been made and as much clarification accomplished as was likely during that round, and that it was appropriate that there be a break, as there had been after the first two rounds, for both parties to study the questions that had surfaced and proposals that had been made. . . .

The two delegations further agreed . . . that when one or the other decided that his own unilateral studies had been carried to the point where resumption of active negotiations together would be profitable, the other party would be notified to that effect through diplomatic channels.

That is where matters stood when the two delegations adjourned by the third round. Now, what in fact happened after that is: Nothing. Nobody deliberately axed the negotiations, nobody scuttled them. . . . My own observation is that basically nothing happened because by that time, which got to be the late part of 1979, the administration at that time was seized with more than it could do on a whole variety of subjects. Afghanistan not being the least, contentions over what to do with the SALT II Treaty being obviously significant, changes of personnel, et cetera. . . .

Now, that is not very spectacular, but that is the objective answer, that just nothing happened.

Senator Pressler. In those talks did you find the Soviets treated the negotiations seriously?

Mr. Buchheim. Very. They fielded an excellent delegation. . . .

Senator Pressler. What I want to know is, did you feel that we had gone forward? Were the Soviets interested in entering into an agreement? I keep hearing from this administration and the past administration that the Soviets would be hard to negotiate with, that they are not particularly interested in this area. Of course, we do not want to enter into a treaty that threatens our national security. I'm not one who totally trusts the Russians.

But it seems that they have taken more initiatives in this area than we have. It seems that the Soviets are more willing, on the face of it, to move toward a treaty or an agreement; would you agree with that assessment?

Mr. Buchheim. Not quite, Mr. Chairman. The fact is that talks on antisatellite matters were initiated at the request of the U.S. Government. We were the ones who exposed that notion to them, and it took them quite a while, during which they asked questions in many ways of many people in the U.S. Government about what our interests were, what our ideas were, until they agreed to start talks.

They did agree to start them and they obviously took them very seriously. Now, the point that you make, that they have been more active than we have, at least in a public way, is true as of relatively recent times.[2]

Although occurring prior to 1981, it seems appropriate to include here the Carter administration's assessment of the 1978–79 negotiations, as explained by General George M. Seignious II, then-director of ACDA, during a Foreign Relations Committee hearing on July 10, 1979: "The United States and the Soviet Union are engaged in negotiations aimed at placing limitations both on attacks against space objects and also on the means to make such attacks.

"The U.S. goal in these negotiations is to prevent an arms race in weapons for attacking space objects. Such a race would increase threats to both sides' satellites, and it would be expensive. The United States would prefer to avoid such a race by negotiating with the Soviet Union equitable limitations on anti-satellite weapons. . . .

"While there remain serious problems, both technical and substantive, for the sides to resolve, I believe it is fair to say we have made progress toward agreement in this area. This is a chance that the arms race in anti-satellite weapons can be avoided."[3]

A slightly different assessment of the 1978–79 talks was given by Dr. Eugene V. Rostow, General Seignious's successor as director of ACDA, at the Foreign Relations Committee hearing on September 20, 1982: "In 1978–79 . . . the United States and the Soviet Union engaged in bilateral negotiations on antisatellite weapons limitations. . . .

"During the first round of negotiations, the two sides outlined their general concerns, and during the second and third rounds some progress was made in examining and clarifying the key issues. However, important areas of disagreement emerged, both with regard to limits on actions against satellites and with regard to limits on ASAT capabilities.

"I do not wish to belabor those differences here. I would note that there were important verification questions raised which must be resolved if ASAT arms control is to make progress. . . .

"We are deeply concerned about the wide-ranging scope of Soviet military activities in space—in particular the continuing Soviet deployment, development and testing of weapons for intercepting and destroying satellites, and the threat posed by Soviet satellites to our own military forces. . . .

"This past June, at nearly the same time that Soviet Foreign Minister Gromyko was speaking before the U.N. about banning weapons from outer space, the Soviet Union was conducting another in a continuing series of tests of its ASAT weapon."[4]

The Soviet attitude toward space arms talks was discussed at a Foreign Relations Committee hearing on April 25, 1984. The following exchange occurred among Senator Claiborne Pell (D-R.I.), head of a delegation of U.S. senators that met in August 1983 with Soviet leader Yuri Andropov; Dr. George Keyworth, President Reagan's science advisor; and Richard Perle, assistant secretary of defense:

Senator Pell. Now, last summer, I was with a group of Senators and we had quite a long discussion of the Soviet leadership with Mr. Andropov. And at that time, he said that the Soviets were willing to dismantle existing ASATs and ban new ones. And as you know, some fear the Soviets would not admit they have their system, and thus would be unwilling to dismantle it. Well, by the very fact of making the offer, they obviously admit that they have the system. . . .

Do you believe the Soviets were prepared to admit they have a system and are prepared to dismantle it?

Dr. Keyworth. I certainly believe the Soviets are prepared to admit they have the system. . . . As far as projecting whether they are willing to abandon it, I certainly cannot. I think it is dangerous to make the assumption. I think that is why we emphasize a reasonable verifiability requirement.

The Soviets did not accompany their proposal, their general proposal, with any specifics on how we could be certain that they would conform. . . .

Senator Pell. I went back to Mr. Andropov three separate times afterward on this question of verifiability. The impression he gave to me was that there would be no real problem with verifiability if we got down to the negotiating stage.

Dr. Keyworth. I am not an expert on arms control negotiations, but I am not the least bit surprised that Mr. Andropov made that suggestion. Nevertheless, the suggestion does not negate the overriding concern at the outset for coupling those discussions with some means by which we can ensure each other that there is some reasonable degree of compliance.

Senator Pell. But isn't it important to at least get into a negotiation and then see on whose back the cat will fall on the question of verifiability, . . . Andropov . . . why not put him to the test? Why do we have this feeling now that we will not deal with him? He made a proposal, and it was made at the United Nations later on, to the effect that they would dismantle their system and engage in a moratorium. . . .

Why is the administration seeking to negotiate all the fringe issues—MBFR [mutually balanced force reduction], chemicals . . . but not willing to get down to the heart of the matter? . . .

Dr. Keyworth. . . . I would just say from first principles that I think each side should enter the negotiations with sincere positions. I would only contend that a position on Mr. Andropov's part that involved an objective, with no attention to the very critical and, I contend—not second order but first order—issue of convincing each other of conformity is not a sincere approach to an arms control negotiation.

Mr. Perle. Senator, the Soviets have a proposed draft treaty on ASAT weapons which provides that verification would be only by national technical means of verification which we and the previous administration have concluded would be hopelessly inadequate.

Senator Pell. Obviously, that is clearly a proposed negotiating position. You go into it, you don't expect your offer that you make—if you are going to buy an automobile, a house, or an arms control treaty—is going to be the final one. The important thing is to get into these negotiations and to get into them before, not after, these weapons are fully developed.

Mr. Perle. It has to have a sound conceptual basis, and we do not know of any way that we could confirm compliance to our own satisfaction.[5]

Soviet sincerity was also examined at a Senate Armed Services Committee hearing on April 12, 1984. Senator John Warner (R-Va.) opened the exchange when he questioned Ambassador Buchheim about the Pressler amendment calling on the president to negotiate a treaty with the Soviets banning space weapons.

Senator Warner. Mr. Buchheim, I am reading an amendment before the Senate which states: "The United States immediately resume negotiations on a mutual and verifiable ban on the testing, production, deployment and use of any antisatellite weapon."

What is your judgment in view of the present Soviet–United States relationship of the immediacy of being able to enter into such talks?

Mr. Buchheim. We should start today, not tomorrow, but today. . . .

Senator Warner. What is the likelihood that the Soviets would respond with equal enthusiasm, in your professional judgment?

Mr. Buchheim. Very good.

Senator Warner. Now, again, the Pressler amendment, I think, could be characterized as calling for a comprehensive agreement.

Do you think that both sides could immediately begin negotiations on a comprehensive agreement banning the production and deployment of antisatellite weapons and any other weapons directed toward space?

Mr. Buchheim. Mr. Chairman, I think we should seek to negotiate as thorough an agreement as we can.

But I don't think we should hold back on negotiating and hopefully putting into place restraints on antisatellite activities and means simply because we can't see what will happen 1,000 years from now.

We should do the best we can. That is all we can do in this world.[6]

Buchheim later added the following comments: "As to whether or not an agreement is reachable with them, again I can only give you an anecdote.

"Three weeks ago in The Netherlands I met with the fellow who was the deputy head of the Soviet delegation in 1978 and 1979. He said some nice things, of course, as they always do, but he also said he has in his own office files of what happened in 1978 and 1979: United States expressions of view, Soviet expressions of view, and their internal analysis of how these compared; and his judgment, which I, frankly, share, was that we were very close to an agreement. We should pick up."[7]

The air force began testing the U.S. ASAT system in January 1984, sparking new congressional debate. The air force tested the rocket on January 21, 1984, and scheduled actual tests against targets in space for later dates. Senator Pell voiced his opposition to the initial test in a floor statement on January 26, 1984: "Mr. President, I was distressed to learn of the first U.S. test on Saturday of a new antisatellite weapon based on an F-15 aircraft.

"On December 21, I wired President Reagan to urge that the test not be conducted. . . . I cautioned him that a test would give the Soviets an excuse to abandon the ASAT moratorium Andropov announced to a Senate delegation I led to the Soviet Union. I expressed my concern that development by both sides of aircraft-based ASATs would jeopardize chances for agreement on a ban and undermine our national security. I have not received a response. However, it is clear now that the advice was not taken.

"The delegation I led is the only congressional delegation Soviet Chairman Yuri Andropov received since taking office. At that session, which lasted nearly 2 hours, he announced new initiatives on ASAT weapons.

"First, he told us, the Soviet Union was declaring a unilateral moratorium on the lauching into space of antisatellite weapons, so long as the United States and other nations also abstained. Second, Mr. Andropov said, the Soviet Union was prepared to dismantle existing ASAT weapons and to ban new ones. . . .

"This was the first time the Soviets had made such an offer. They had never before shown any interest in dismantling their own system, and they had avoided any reference to an ASAT ban in their 1981 draft treaty submitted to the United Nations.

". . . Unfortunately, the administration is simply not interested in actively seeking a ban on ASAT weapons. The oft-expressed need for verification is being used by some as an excuse for doing nothing. I recognize the importance of verification, and I questioned Chairman Andropov about his willingness to agree to effective verification. He seemed forthcoming. It seems to me that the smart approach would be to open bilateral negotiations so that we can put the Soviet initiative to the test. Nothing but disaster can be gained by continued inaction."[8]

Ambassador Buchheim expressed a different view, supportive of U.S. ASAT tests. This exchange took place during the Senate Armed Service Committee hearing on April 12, 1984.

[*Senator Jeff Bingaman* (D-N.M.).] . . . One of the other statements I understand the administration to be making is that we would expect to go ahead and test our satellite capability, this homing device, in the fall.

Assuming that there is no legislative obstacle to that, to what extent would that action or further development or testing of ours impair our ability to reach any meaningful arms control in this area?

Are we in a very time-sensitive situation where there is an opportunity for significant arms control which will be significantly reduced in the future?

Mr. Buchheim. In my opinion, sir, the answer is no. If we go ahead with our test program, nothing is going to change that has had any significance and, in my opinion, we should go ahead with our test program.

I think the last thing the United States needs is to address this question in the next several years in the absence of any knowledge as to whether our preferred system will work or not.

That seems to me a very poor way to leapfrog.

Yes, test it; let's find out. If it works, fine, that is fine. That is contingency one.

If it doesn't work, that is contingency two.

I don't think we should stop.[9]

General Charles A. Gabriel, chief of staff of the air force, was among the officials who testified that a tested U.S. ASAT would be a valuable bargaining chip. Following are statements he made at a House Appropriations Committee hearing on March 6, 1984: " It is a matter of tactics I think as to how we get this negotiation with the other side going. As soon as we get something that we can say has a capability. . . .

"They have said . . . 'Let us ban ASATs' but we have talked to them about this. They wanted to capture the space shuttle in the negotiations because it maneuvers a little bit. I think that it would pay us to investigate the possibilities of ASAT negotiations but we must be cautious of what is included in such negotiations. Once we demonstrate an ASAT capability, we will be in a more reasonable position to execute realistic negotiations. Like the ABM, the treaty, they did not negotiate seriously at all until we got some capability and then they sat down and talked."[10]

In the same hearing, under questioning by Representative Norman D. Dicks (D-Wash.), General Gabriel said the air force would ban all ASATs, if possible.

Mr. Dicks. Dr. DeLauer is quoted as stating that you are studying options for an advanced ASAT system that could attack higher altitude satellites. . . .

A system capable of attacking high-altitude targets would obviously threaten early warning and attack assessment assets. Such a capability would have obvious major implications on stability. Even T.K. Jones [deputy under-secretary of defense] has said to me that such a capability would not serve our best interests. How would you anticipate utilizing such a system, would it be part of a decapitating strike capability?

General Gabriel. I would not anticipate using it nor would I recommend that we build such a system. I would rather both sides not have a capability to go to geosynchronous with an ASAT. In fact I would like to be able to agree with the Soviets that we not have any ASATs if we could verify it properly. Because we are an open society, we need our space capabilities more than they do.[11]

ASAT weapons and space-based BMDs are related technologies. Thus, an ASAT ban would limit the administration's options for developing a space-based BMD. This contradiction was the subject of a discussion during a Foreign Relations Committee hearing on April 25, 1984, between Dr. George Keyworth, President Reagan's science advisor, and Senator Charles H. Percy (R-Ill.), then-chairman of the committee.

Dr. Keyworth. . . . In order to leave our successors any options at all [for BMD], we cannot tie our hands now. While I see absolutely no need to violate any provisions on existing treaties while we investigate these options, I am very leery of entangling ourselves in further constraints until we know more. . . .

Senator Percy. Is this the real reason that the administration refuses to enter into ASAT negotiations—not verification as the administration report suggests—because if this is true, then it would mean that we really could not get into these negotiations for at least 5 years?

Dr. Keyworth. No, no. Senator Percy, the reasons have been clearly stated in the President's policy that was submitted to Congress on March 31, and I endorse those views entirely. I was simply addressing the Strategic Defense Initiative as a research project that I believe is extremely important to our ultimate posture and strategy and future options, and that those options should not be constrained.

So I guess I was addressing the Strategic Defense Initiative specifically. And if you move it into the context of the committee's concerns about ASAT, I entirely support the policy and the exact comments that Richard Perle has been making about verifiability. . . . We have not . . . found an approach or a potential treaty that holds significant merit.[12]

The Senate Foreign Relations Committee issued a November 18, 1983, report strongly urging an ASAT ban and continued adherence to the ABM treaty.[13] That report offered the following recommendations and analysis: "The Committee believes that the 1977 decision to pursue the F-15 ASAT system primarily to bring about an agreement involving the dismantlement of the Soviet ASAT, was based on sound judgment. . . .

"The Committee strongly urges that the President take three actions if an arms race in space is to be avoided. First, immediately seek a mutual and verifiable moratorium of limited duration on ASAT space flight tests. This would sustain conditions required for quickly reaching a mutual and verifiable ban on all ASAT weapons. Under this arrangement the Soviets would have incentives for seeking agreement since the U.S. would retain its option to deploy the F-15 ASAT if the Soviets prove uncompromising. Second, immediately resume bilateral negotiations to prohibit the testing, production, deployment, and use of any antisatellite weapon. This is the best method available to determine whether the Soviets wish to avoid a space weapons competition. If an accord can be reached it would eliminate the Soviet ASAT threat and prevent a costly and potentially dangerous space arms race. Third, these talks should be urgently expanded to include negotiations on all future space-based and space-directed weaponry. This would reinforce and expand the prohibitions contained in the ABM Treaty, an accord which has clearly served U.S. security interests.

"Earlier accords such as the treaty establishing a nuclear-free zone in Latin America, the Outer Space Treaty, the Antarctic Treaty and the Seabed Arms Control Treaty have served to prohibit weapons before their deployment in specific zones. The Environmental Modification Treaty has served to prohibit the use of a class of weapons. There may be an opportunity now to stop ASATs before either side has a significant system and to ban space-based and space-directed weapons before they are impossible to stop. We can reap the enormous benefits of such achievements if we are willing to treat obstacles to agreement not as insurmountable barriers but as challenges to be met directly and overcome. We would do well to follow the example of President Kennedy, who, during the Cuban Missile Crisis, seized on the positive—rather than the unacceptable—aspects of the Soviet position and built toward a successful resolution."

In the Fiscal Year 1984 Defense Appropriations Act, Congress required the administration to submit a full report on U.S. ASAT arms control policy. President Reagan submitted the report on its due date, March 31, 1984. It concluded that a verifiable ASAT agreement was not possible and that none could be found that would be in the national interest.

"No arrangements or agreements beyond those already governing military activities in outer space have been found to date that are judged to be in the overall interest of the United States and its Allies," President Reagan said in his cover letter for the report. He added that unless effective ASAT arms control measures could be identified, "I do not believe it would be productive to engage in formal international negotiations."[14]

Subsequent congressional arms control debate combined with a tide of criticism from experts led to a shift in administration policy, and in the summer of 1984 President Reagan indicated his willingness to place space weaponry on the agenda for renewed arms talks with the Soviets.

The March 31 report, however, remains the most comprehensive explanation to date of the administration's stand on the ASAT issue. In essence, the administration made two principal arguments to support its delay in resuming bilateral talks on a space arms ban. One held that significant verification problems would make it difficult, if not impossible, to determine whether the Soviets were complying with a ban on space arms. The other maintained that the United States requires an ASAT for strategic reasons.

The report's conclusion that ASAT limits cannot be verified was to be expected. Government specialists who prepared the analysis had been directed to consider a "comprehensive" ASAT ban. As a result, they identified not only significant threats to U.S. satellites, but also the most unlikely dangers to U.S. space assets. At least one of the threats identified—that of space mines—is probably remote, according to a study by OTA.[15]

The administration's report cited the verification problems presented by residual ASAT threats, such as the potential for transforming a satellite into an ASAT by rigging it with explosives. Some have argued that if residual delivery capabilities were factors in nuclear arms control talks, there would be no hope of limiting nuclear weapons until all commercial airlines were banned. Any airliner could be used to deliver a nuclear bomb.

The administration also contended that all verification issues should be resolved before the United States entered into space arms negotiations. Many considered this an unrealistic premise. The United States entered into Strategic Arms Reduction Talks and Intermediate-Range Nuclear Forces Talks before all verification problems were settled. Many remain unresolved. It is argued that only by negotiating face-to-face with the Soviets can one hope to learn what arms control verification measures are possible.

A panel that met in Washington in January 1984 to explore space weapons and arms control possibilities generally disagreed with the pessimism of the administration about verification. The panel was organized by OTA. McGeorge Bundy, President Kennedy's national security advisor, served as chairman. Other panelists included both opponents and proponents of space arms control from U.S. nuclear weapons laboratories, defense industries, strategic think tanks, and universities. This group concluded that some ASAT arms control provisions could be verified with "high confidence" and that ASAT arms control could "serve to lessen the measures required to protect space systems."[16]

Several analysts on the panel asserted that a verifiable accord could be reached that would actually reduce the most direct threats to U.S. satellites. They maintained that the existing Soviet ASAT is associated with a few known SS-9 launch facilities. If the Soviets dismantled the SS-9 launch pads, they would be unable to launch their ASAT from the one booster with which it has been tested. Destruction of these launch facilities could be monitored by national technical means of verification. It might be impossible to prevent the Soviets from secretly producing and hiding their ASAT interceptors, but these would be harmless without the tested launchers.

These analysts also stressed that limits on the Soviet Union's high-energy laser tests could be effectively verified. At present, the limited Soviet high-energy laser facilities pose only a potential threat to U.S. satellites. Without restrictions, however, the Soviets will improve their high-energy lasers until they become a real threat to the United States' most important early warning and communications satellites. By limiting high-energy laser tests, advanced development of these systems might be restrained.

An ASAT accord could also prevent the Soviet nuclear-tipped Galosh ABM system around Moscow from becoming a major threat to U.S. satellites. This system, which is limited to 100 interceptors, is permitted by the 1972 ABM treaty. Its primary role is antimissile defense. At present, its potential against satellites is limited, since an attack on U.S. satellites with nuclear explosives would also destroy Soviet satellites in the vicinity. Testing of the ABM system in an ASAT mode could, however, lead to improvements in accuracy. And with improved accuracy Galosh might become an effective, conventionally armed ASAT weapon that posed no threats to nearby Soviet satellites.

If an accord could eliminate the Soviet Union's dedicated ASAT and strictly limit the ASAT potential of embedded Soviet systems, other threats to U.S. satellites could be met with survivability measures. Without such a ban and limitations, survivability measures may be of little value.

Many of the obstacles to ASAT arms control that the administration cited in its March 31 report were also challenged by a number of other experts in a widely quoted article published in *Science* magazine on May 18, 1984.[17] The author, R. Jeffrey Smith, based the article on personal interviews and congressional testimony.

Some of the challenges, as reported by Smith, were as follows: James Reynolds, a leading satellite program manager currently with Northrop Corporation and formerly with the Air Force Space Division, took issue with the administration's contention that space mines are significant and unverifiable ASAT threats. In theory, space mines are covertly deployed, miniature killer satellites. But Reynolds believes they exist only in the minds of ASAT arms control opponents. "The people who postulate this threat don't know a spacecraft from a frying pan," Reynolds asserted.

Dr. Michael May, associate director of Lawrence Livermore National Laboratory, challenged the report's conclusion that low-powered lasers are unverifiable threats to satellites. These would be effective against U.S. satellites only if U.S. designers were "remarkably careless" and failed to provide countermeasures, Dr. May said. He also had a different assessment of high-powered lasers. The March 31 report said these would be hard to detect. Dr. May asserted, "The installation of high-powered laser systems would be detectable."

Leslie Dirks of the Raytheon Corporation and a former Central Intelligence Agency (CIA) deputy director for research and technology felt the report overstated the problems of verifying ASAT tests. "I'm quite confident that testing things surreptitiously in space is a hard thing to do, and the United States has a very robust detection capability in this area," Dirks stated. He also questioned the administration's misgivings about covertly developed and untested ASATs. "I know that the Soviet military would be very unwilling to depend on a system that has not been fully tested," he told *Science.*

What about the administration's fears that peaceful space systems might be converted into ASAT systems? Walter Slocombe, who headed the SALT task force in the Carter administration's Pentagon, saw this as a minor threat, at best. "In a crisis involving low-level U.S.–Soviet hostilities, only high confidence, high precision ASAT systems would suffice. Jury-rigged systems are clearly inadequate," he insisted.

Other congressional arms control hearings in 1984 produced still more viewpoints, pro and con, concerning the administration's controversial report.

Richard Perle, assistant secretary of defense, spoke for the administration during a meeting of the Foreign Relations Committee on April 25, 1984. Senator John Glenn (D-Ohio) asked Perle why the administration was reluctant to negotiate an ASAT ban when it was willing to negotiate "a ban on chemical weapons which are far more difficult to verify than anything to do with ASATs."[18]

"Senator," Perle replied, "I disagree about the difficulties of verification. There are a variety of means, about a dozen or so, by which the Soviets could hope to attack and either destroy or destroy the effectiveness of our satellites. Many of these involve technologies that have other applications, and verification includes more than the observance of activity. It involves the ability to reach a judgment that that activity is prohibited because it constitutes a violation of an agreement. . . .

"The difficulty there is that a small violation of an ASAT ban would have immense military consequences. . . . [But] hiding . . . a relatively small number of chemical weapons . . . would not be of such decisive consequences. The situations are really not comparable."

Among the major critics of the administration's report were William E. Colby, former director of the CIA, and Gerard Smith, chief of the U.S. delegation to SALT from 1969 to 1972.

Testifying at a Foreign Relations Committee hearing on June 13, 1984, Colby said the ability to verify an ASAT ban is demonstrated by the fact that the United States already knows a great deal about the Soviet ASAT program.[19] "What we know about the Soviet ASAT system did not come from any announcement by Moscow. We discovered this through our intelligence systems," Colby testified. "We are going to continue to verify Soviet development of nuclear weaponry, whether there is ever a treaty between us or not. The only difference is that these kinds of treaties make the process a lot easier, and therefore the idea of a comprehensive ban on the development of new ASAT weapons I think would certainly be reasonably verifiable to the extent necessary to protect our nation's security."

Testifying at a hearing by the House Committee on Foreign Affairs on June 21, 1984, Gerard Smith said that "under appropriate procedures, any technology can be verified. . . . My feeling is that we should engage the Soviets promptly in discussions as to what is possible and what is not possible in controlling ASATs. I am not of the belief that we are going to negotiate a treaty this year or maybe in 2 years, but I think we have a lot to learn about it."[20]

The administration's argument for development of a U.S. ASAT was based on the need for deterrence and defense. Regarding deterrence, the report stated: "If, for example, during a crisis or conflict, the Soviet Union were to destroy a U.S. satellite, the United States would lack the capability to respond in kind to avoid escalating the conflict. Thus, in present circumstances a U.S. capability to destroy satellites clearly responds to the need to deter such Soviet attacks."[21] Regarding defense, the report argued that the U.S. ASAT was needed to initiate attacks on Soviet surveillance satellites that can target U.S. ground-based forces.

As for the deterrence argument, the Senate Foreign Relations Committee noted that the United States is more dependent upon satellites for defense than is the Soviet Union. "To a high degree, the U.S. must rely upon satellites for effective command and control of U.S. forces in many situations where the Soviets possess land-lines to perform these functions," the report pointed out.[22] It noted that "trends point to increasing U.S. dependence on space-based systems for military activities."

"Under these conditions of greater and increasing U.S. dependence on space systems, a U.S.–Soviet satellite exchange employing ASAT weapons will likely be far more disruptive of U.S. military activities on earth. . . . On the other hand, a ban of all ASATs would deprive the Soviets of an effective attack capability, whatever the level of relative dependence on space systems," the committee report concluded.

The committee found the administration's defense rationale to be inconsistent. It noted, "The U.S. may elect to initiate satellite attacks to neutralize threats posed by Soviet space surveillance systems used to direct Soviet forces against U.S. forces. . . . At a minimum, this argument contradicts the deterrence justification for the U.S. ASAT program."

The committee observed that "aside from this inconsistency, there are other considerations which suggest that the military threat posed by these Soviet systems is not in and of itself so significant as to stand in the way of arms control efforts to make space a sanctuary."

The Senate–House compromise on space weapons and arms control, passed in October 1984, tied ASAT tests to arms control efforts, as the Pressler amendment proposed. It also limited ASAT tests to three in 1985 and delayed these tests until March 1985. Late in February, the administration voluntarily postponed further tests until June 1985, in a move many felt was intended to improve the atmosphere for renewed nuclear arms reduction negotiations between the superpowers.

The hearings and other proceedings described in this chapter, as well as the extended deliberations over the early ASAT resolutions, set the stage for full-fledged debates in the House and Senate over ASAT limitations.

4

The House Debates
Antisatellite Systems

On May 23, 1984, three weeks before the Senate debated the Pressler and Tsongas resolutions, a lively exchange began in the House of Representatives over a proposed moratorium on the testing of the U.S. ASAT system.

At issue was an amendment by Congressman George Brown (D-Calif.), a member of the House Science and Technology Committee and a leading advocate of space arms control. The Brown amendment called for a ban on U.S. ASAT tests against a target in space unless or until the Soviet Union resumed testing its ASAT weapon. This, in effect, would extend the one-year moratorium on U.S. ASAT tests imposed in July 1983 with passage of the Tsongas amendment.

Sharp opposition to the Brown amendment was voiced by Congressman Ken Kramer (R-Colo.), a leading advocate of space-based defenses and the author of the People Protection Act (H.R. 3073).

As others joined in, the House debate grew into a full-scale deliberation about ASAT technology, the relationship of ASATs to BMDs, and the question of whether the United States would be more or less secure if an effective ASAT ban could be imposed on both the United States and the Soviet Union. When a final vote was taken, the Brown amendment passed by a decisive 238 to 181.

Representative Brown had tried in May 1983 to slow the pace of ASAT development with an amendment to delete all funding ($19 million) for procurement of ASAT weapons. The measure would have left untouched $209 million for ASAT research and development. But the 1983 Brown amendment was defeated by 177 to 243, perhaps because the House had not yet held extensive hearings on space weapons and space arms control.[1] The first resolution on these subjects was introduced in the House in September 1982 (H.J.

Res. 607). The first House hearing on space weapons took place on November 10, 1983, five months after the vote on the first Brown amendment.[2]

By May 1984 the climate had changed. Deployment of space weapons had become a major issue in the House. ASATs were regarded by some not as just another weapons program but as sophisticated space-based weapons that could precipitate a new arms race between the superpowers.

Representative Brown offered his 1984 ASAT amendment during House debate on the Defense Department authorization bill for fiscal year 1985 (H.R. 5167). During the preceding year, the Soviets had declared a unilateral ban on ASAT testing and had presented to the United Nations a draft treaty for the dismantling of ASAT systems. The Soviet ASAT had already been tested 20 times.

Brown observed: "[The] amendment continues for one more year the existing moratorium on the testing of antisatellite weapons by. . . the Soviets and the United States.

"The Soviets have not tested their antisatellite weapon in the past two years. Because of . . .the so-called Tsongas amendment, which was put in on the Senate side, the United States has not tested its antisatellite weapon.

"My amendment, very simply, continues this situation. It says as long as the Soviets do not continue to test, that we will not continue to test."[3] Brown said the Soviet ASAT was comparable to a "Model T," while the U.S. ASAT, by contrast, was a "Model A." But he noted that the United States has a number of "Cadillac" ASATs in the research stage, which could be deployed "in the not too distant future."

Brown reminded his colleagues that his 1983 amendment to deny funds for ASAT procurement had been defeated and that Congress instead had approved the Tsongas amendment, imposing a one-year ASAT ban. "So this year it was my thought that instead of trying to strike the fund for the procurement of the system itself that we would continue the moratorium in the hopes that the administration might be willing to accept this as a way of saving money, if nothing else, and that it might be willing to go back to discussions with the Soviets about not deploying an antisatellite system on either side and, in fact, destroying the present systems that may exist."

"It was my view," he continued, ". . . that if they delay testing a little bit longer, that the realities of the fiscal picture, if nothing else, will catch up with them. This is not a high priority system. It is one with huge costs down the road. And if they are forced into a situation where

there has to be some cap on military spending, this system will probably be the first one to go. Therefore, if we can delay further
testing . . .there will be no great loss to anybody when the time
comes to make the necessary decisions with regard to financing this
system."

Kramer, noting that he had "problems" with the Brown amendment, took the floor: "First, let me say that I am troubled by the
trend that I see on the House floor to abrogate our own respon-
sibilities of meeting our vital security interests, especially in cases
where tremendous disparity exists between the United States, as it
does in the case of the Soviets' predominance in the field of ASATs,
where we have no capability, and then in effect allowing the Soviet
Union unilaterally to decide the course of action on whether or not
we are going to have programs like the MX, and so forth, and
especially in this case, like ASAT.

"Because as I read your amendment, . . . as long as the Soviet
Union continues to refrain from future testing, discounting all the
past testing they have done, the 20-odd tests that they have run, 9 of
which at least are successful in terms of having kills, we will
restrain ourselves unilaterally from going forward to build an
equality in our capabilities. . . .

"It disturbs me that we leave the Soviets, in effect, with not only
preeminence in this field, but with total domination. . . .

"In fact, most of the rest of our space-borne assets, everything
out to about 3,000 miles is put at risk by the Soviet system, and
under the gentleman's agreement, we would not, in effect, make up
this discrepancy."

Brown challenged Kramer's assertion that the Soviets have "an
operational [ASAT] system of high effectiveness." "I indicated in my
opening remarks that theirs is a Model T system: that it is not of
high effectiveness," he argued. "We had this same debate last year.
You know, poor, helpless America at the mercy of this great
sophisticated system."

Brown referred his colleagues to an article from a leading
aerospace magazine describing 25 years of U.S. ASAT testing and
the deployment of an ASAT system during the 1964–75 period. "We
had deployed, operated, a system with the same capability that they
have today, 15 years ago, and we scrapped it," he said. "What we
have today and are still working on, we demonstrated would work
20 years ago." Brown insisted that the United States is not in the
"posture of technological inferiority."

Addressing Kramer, Brown added: "The gentleman knows, as
do other members of the Armed Services Committee, that we are

spending literally billions of dollars on testing the next generation of ASAT which will have far more capability than this crude, kinetic weapon on which it is proposed to spend somewhere between $3.5 and $15 billion.

"I am making this argument to appeal to those of you who want the best possible ASAT weapon. I do not happen to want any; I would prefer to keep arms out of space, but the practical reality is that we have in being right now systems which probably can be deployed within 5 to 10 years that are far superior to this system that we are proposing to spend . . .somewhere between $3.5 and $15 billion on."

Congresswoman Marilyn Lloyd (D-Tenn.), a member of the House Armed Services Committee, rose to oppose the Brown amendment on the grounds that it would hinder U.S. research and development of "promising" BMD systems. "The antisatellite (ASAT) systems are strongly linked to star wars technologies," she said. "I am afraid the gentleman's agreement, though well-intended, actually undermines the U.S. capability to perform research, development, testing and evaluation (RDT&E) of promising BMD systems and muddies the water in terms of our ability to develop such stabilizing systems from an arms control perspective."

Representative Lawrence Coughlin (R-Penn.) then observed: "This amendment does not cut off any funding for ASAT system development. . . . This amendment does not prevent the testing of an ASAT by the United States. The amendment only prevents the testing of an ASAT against an object in space, unless the President certifies that the Soviets have tested an ASAT.

"Under this amendment, an ASAT still could be built, it still could be tested against a point in space. . . .

"Once the United States achieves an operational ASAT system by testing against a target in space, the Soviets will almost certainly abandon their 2-year-old ASAT testing moratorium in order to begin development of a more advanced system. At present the Soviets have a primitive ASAT system using a modified SS-9 missile to place a satellite interceptor in orbit. . . . It can be fairly inexpensively countered by various survivability measures—hardening of our own satellites, increasing their maneuverability, or by using decoys and spares for quick relaunch.

"Although the crude Soviet ASAT system has been judged operational, it has not been tested for nearly 2 years and poses a potential threat to only a relatively small number of low-orbit weather reconnaissance, electronic intelligence and 9 navigation satellites. Most of our militarily significant satellites that would be critical in time of international crisis are in geosynchronous orbit at altitudes well beyond present Soviet ASAT capabilities. Those few low-orbit U.S. satellites that serve important military purposes are being moved to high orbits out of range of present Soviet ASATs.

"However, in the absence of a mutual ban on testing ASATs the Soviets can be counted on to develop a whole new generation of ASATs designed to match or surpass our own current technology. It will then be only a matter of time before our vital high-altitude satellites used for early warning, nuclear attack assessment, military communications, and arms control verification will become vulnerable to Soviet ASAT attack."

Coughlin quoted from a letter he had received from Gerard C. Smith, arms control advisor to seven presidents and a chief architect of SALT I. Smith wrote, in part: "I have long been concerned about the threat that antisatellite weapons pose to military satellites and, therefore, to strategic stability. I also believe that most experts are convinced that the United States is substantially more dependent on the continued integrity of its military satellites than is the U.S.S.R. Therefore, I believe that a mutual moratorium on testing satellite killers clearly would be in the security interests of the United States."

Coughlin also quoted from a report by the House Foreign Affairs Subcommittee on International Security and Scientific Affairs, which warned, "An increase in both United States and Soviet ASAT capabilities . . . may well prove unavoidable, if efforts to limit these weapons are not mutually made by both superpowers."

A number of Republican representatives, who favored the administration's plans to continue ASAT testing, questioned whether the Soviets were actually observing an ASAT moratorium.

Congressman Gerald B. H. Solomon (R-N.Y.) complained that if the Brown amendment passed it would stalemate the president's SDI. Congressman William S. Broomfield (R-Mich.) argued that the administration's ASAT program was a necessary response to the growing Soviet military space threat. "An arms race in space was instigated years ago as a result of Soviet strategic space operations, including the testing of ASATs in space in the 1970s and early 1980s, the deployment of nearly four times the number of spacecraft as the United States, most of which have military applications, the recent testing of a space plane, the deployment of seven space stations in orbit since 1971, most of which have military reconnaissance capabilities, the development of a new super-booster rocket designed to launch larger payloads including space stations and spaceborne lasers, and the continuing development of laser and particle beam armaments," Broomfield pointed out.

Several supporters of the Brown amendment attacked the "hidden and escalating costs" associated with the U.S. ASAT system. Addressing this problem, Congressman John Joseph Moakley (D-Mass.) noted: "The recent selected acquisitions review report, put out by the Department of Defense, showed a $300 million increase in the cost of the ASAT program—from $3.6 to $3.9 billion. And there is a General Accounting Office report that estimates the total cost of the U.S. ASAT to be in the 'tens of billions of dollars'. And that is just the tip of the iceberg. More grandiose space weaponry could cost in the trillions of dollars."

Other arguments focused on the problems of ASAT verification and the fact that the United States is more dependent on satellites than is the Soviet Union for vital communications, navigation, intelligence, and treaty verification purposes.

Moakley noted that the new F-15-launched U.S. ASAT would be "a verification nightmare" because of its small size, "thus precluding the chance for a future agreement banning ASATs."

"Once the U.S. weapon is fully tested, every F-15 will be a potential ASAT platform in Soviet eyes," he said. "In contrast to the current Soviet system, the American system could threaten crucial Soviet communications and early warning satellites. Thus, if we are truly concerned about arms control, it is imperative that we immediately halt any further ASAT testing."

A number of Democrats charged that the administration wanted to deploy ASATs in order to develop space-based BMDs that would bypass the 1972 ABM treaty. This issue was the subject of an exchange, at one point, between Congressman Thomas J. Bliley, Jr. (R-Va.) and Congressman Norman D. Dicks (D-Wash.). In an impassioned speech, Bliley described President Reagan's SDI as "one of the most important steps toward the future peace of the world in the last 20 years." Without an effective defense system, Bliley said, this country could respond to a ballistic missile attack in only one of two ways: by launching a retaliatory strike and starting World War III or by doing nothing and letting our cities and population be destroyed. This dialogue followed:

Mr. Bliley. The strategic defense initiative presents a third choice—a choice that does not automatically doom millions to certain death. . . .

Many Members would have us believe that a strategic defense is too dangerous. But, I ask you, where is that danger? How can a purely defensive system endanger any but an attacking enemy?

Mr. Dicks. Is the gentleman suggesting that the antisatellite system has a defensive capability against strategic missiles?

Mr. Bliley. I think that the research and development that goes into it will provide the information that helps us develop a system that will provide the strategic defense.

Mr. Dicks. Is the gentleman suggesting that one of the reasons why the administration may want to do all this R&D on antisatellite systems is because it gives them a chance to develop systems that would be necessary for a strategic defense initiative?

Mr. Bliley. It may not develop the specific system, but it certainly gives them the basic research that will be necessary.

Congressman Mel Levine (D-Calif.) had more direct criticism: "In its zeal to move ahead with deployment of ASATs and a space-based ballistic missile system, this administration has ignored our Nation's long-standing policy commitment to preserve space as a peaceful sanctuary. For example, the 1972 ABM Treaty prohibits development and deployment of a space based BMD system," he argued.

"However, because the technologies associated with development of ASATs and a BMD defense shield are closely linked, this administration could claim that its space shield weapon is part of an ASAT program, which is not restricted by any treaty, thus bypassing the ABM Treaty. Therefore, under the guise of pursuing a limited ASAT program, this administration could begin to pursue a course of weaponizing space that would ultimately prompt a more fierce phase in the arms race on Earth and in space."

Levine complained that because the administration "is opposed to negotiating with the U.S.S.R.," Congress had been forced to call attention to the urgent need for negotiations on an ASAT ban. He further asserted that, contrary to the administration's position, verification of ASAT testing was possible. "Just as the United States has closely monitored Soviet ASAT tests in space—and has learned that many of these tests have been unsuccessful—it will continue to monitor such tests in the future," he said.

Congressman John F. Seiberling (D-Ohio) avowed that "bipartisan and widespread" support in the House for the Brown amendment, which he cosponsored, was "a clear indication that concern about the lack of progress on arms control for space weapons, and concern about the impending arms race in space, is growing in this body." He also asserted that verification was feasible, but warned this would not be true once the United States tested its ASAT against a target in space.

Congressman Mervyn M. Dymally (D-Calif.) drew an analogy between the 1984 House debate on ASATs and the congressional debate over MIRVs 15 years earlier. He recalled that in the late 1960s the

United States proceeded with the development of the MIRVs because they offered the promise of "transforming the targeting power of the U.S. nuclear arsenal." "By placing MIRVs on our land- and sea-based missiles, we would greatly multiply the numbers of deliverable nuclear warheads without having to build so many additional missiles," Dymally said. Many experts warned Congress that if the Soviets developed their own MIRVs, they could—given the large size of their ICBMs—put many more warheads atop each missile than could the United States, he recalled.

Dymally quoted a "prophetic statement" made during congressional testimony in 1970 by Marshall D. Shulman, then-director of the Columbia University Russian Institute. Shulman testified: "If we fail to hold the line on MIRV, Minuteman seems destined for obsolescence in the foreseeable future. . . . We will both be obliged, certainly by the time the second generation of MIRVs makes its appearance, to enter upon a huge restructuring of our strategic forces to protect ourselves from the vulnerabilities to which MIRV will subject us."

As Dymally summarized subsequent events, MIRVs were not stopped during the SALT I talks, and both nations pushed ahead with this system for expanding their nuclear arsenals. The Soviets caught up with the United States, then gained effective superiority by putting MIRVs on larger missiles. And, as Shulman and others had predicted, the United States found it would have to restructure its forces to get rid of the vulnerability problem created by Soviet MIRVing.

"If we had prevented the Soviets from developing MIRVs by not pushing ahead with them ourselves, then maybe we wouldn't have had to engage in the lengthy and difficult MX debate over the past few years," Dymally said. "And maybe we would not now be faced with the difficult problem of trying to figure out how to get from our present world of MIRVed ICBMs to a world of small, single warhead ICBMs such as the Midgetman.

"Nobody knows whether or not we could have stopped MIRVs back then. Partly because we hardly attempted to do so. But that is no reason for not trying to stop ASATs today."

Dymally was one of several representatives who warned that the Soviets could repeat their MIRV feat by catching up with, then leapfrogging, the U.S. ASAT effort, ultimately threatening the United States' early warning and communications satellites.

Several Republican representatives took issue with those who described the Soviet system as "primitive." Ken Kramer was the chief spokesperson on this point: "All this talk about the Soviet system being so primitive, that it is bow and arrow, a model T system, is just so much balderdash.

"The facts truly speak for themselves. They have made 14 tests. We know they have had nine successful kills. We know that even on the five tests that were not verified as kills, we are not sure that they were trying to get kills. In fact, they might have just been product development tests. . . .

"Their present capability is such that it totally threatens our reconnaissance capability. That is not a primitive system. . . . That is a system that they incorporated in a first strike exercise . . . a year and one-half ago which started with an ASAT test. . . .

"While I deeply believe in arms control . . . I do not believe that unilateral disarmament, going to the Soviet Union in supplication, asking them to talk with us, is a good national strategy, one that serves this country well."

Congressman John Edward Porter (R-Ill.) took the floor to complain that he took "umbrage" at suggestions that representatives who favored the Brown amendment were against all weapons and in favor of unilateral disarmament. "I have supported the MX, the B-1B, the Trident, the Pershing II and a number of other weapons systems. I think what we really require today is some thoughtful approaches to our military requirements. We obviously cannot afford everything on the military shelf. . . .

Antisatellite weaponry is an area, it seems to me, that could be so costly to both sides that we should find a way if we can, reasonably, to avoid building new systems."

Porter said the Brown amendment offered a "very ingenious approach" because it allowed a de facto agreement, without negotiations, that could forestall ASAT development by both the United States and the Soviet Union.

Kramer was not convinced. "Let us not be naive in believing that the Soviets do not think of space as the ultimate area to gain strategic supremacy, because they do," he asserted. "Make no doubt about it."

Kramer quoted from *Military Thought,* a Soviet military publication, which stated that "the mastering of space is a prerequisite for achieving victory in war." "That is precisely how they look at their ASAT and every other system that they are building," said Kramer. "And, believe me, there are other systems that they are building, and, in fact, have already built. They have a Galosh ABM system with nuclear warhead, which could be used in ASAT mode. Present U.S. capability, zero. They are today spending three to five times in directed energy research and development what we are in this country. In fact, today, as we meet in this chamber, they now have at Sary Shagan two ground-based lasers that give them the current technical capability to blind our own satellite optical systems well beyond low orbit."

Congressman Albert Gore (D-Tenn.), who was elected to the Senate in 1984, said this inventory of weapons illustrated the need for an agreement to stop the spiraling arms race in space. "The only way we are going to deal with this problem is through an arms control agreement. If we continually try to leapfrog the Soviet Union and they continually try to leapfrog us, we are going to move away from stability and spiral toward a hair trigger situation," he said. This dialogue followed Gore's statement:

Mr. Kramer. I would be more than happy to sit down with the Soviets and talk to them about the full panoply of strategic and factual issues, including weapons in outer space.

Mr. Gore. But the administration is not willing to.

Mr. Kramer. That is not the issue here in front of us today.

Mr. Gore. But the administration has said it will not even talk to them about this subject.

Mr. Kramer. The issue here on this floor today is twofold. No. 1, Brown does allow research and development, but it prevents us from getting to an operational capability comparable to the Soviets. And it also approaches arms control aspirations and hopes in terms of further unilateral restraint by this country.

This history of arms control since SALT I has been: We restrain; they build. They build regardless of what we do, whether we build, whether we do something in between, or whether we totally stop. And what I am suggesting here today is that while we should indeed sit down with the Soviet Union and find a way out of the . . . nuclear dilemma . . . we cannot solve that problem today. The only issue that we can solve here on the floor today is whether or not unilateral restraint will get us the operational capability that we need for Soviet–United States comparability in ASAT, and it will not.

Another Democrat, Congressman Robert J. Mrazek (D-N.Y.), bristled at Kramer's suggestion that supporters of the Brown amendment favored unilateral disarmament. "It seems to me that after I have voted for $270 billion worth of defense authorization and defense appropriations bills, and we are moving forward with an MX missile, a Pershing missile, the ground-launched, sea-launched, air-launched cruise missiles, the Midgetman missile, the Star Wars program, a rapid deployment force, a larger standing Army, going from 4 divisions to 5 in Western Europe, a 600-ship Navy and a whole host of other things including 4 more World War II vintage battleships, no one could suggest that the U.S. Government is thinking about unilateral disarmament," he argued.

Two other amendments were offered during the May 23, 1984, House debate on Brown's ASAT testing moratorium amendment. One by Representative Dave McCurdy (D-Okla.) called for a six-month ban on ASAT tests, after which the administration could proceed with testing if the president had developed an arms control program and had invited the Soviets to begin ASAT talks. McCurdy said his measure would serve as an incentive to the Soviets to pursue arms control because only by so doing could they block U.S. ASAT tests. Opponents argued, however, that the McCurdy amendment "while well-intentioned" would allow the administration to go forward with tests in six months. The amendment was defeated by a vote of 186 to 228.

The second amendment, by Congresswoman Beverly B. Byron (D-Md.), would have allowed the United States to test its ASAT as often as the Soviet Union had tested its system. The United States would then refrain from further tests as long as the Soviet Union did likewise.

Byron said she was sympathetic to the Brown amendment. "However, we cannot ignore the fact that the Soviet Union has the world's only ASAT system," she said. "Moreover . . . the Soviets have . . . satellites designed to locate our ships and transmit this information to submarines and aircraft to permit them to attack at large standoff distances, hundreds of miles, with cruise missiles."

Congressman Norman D. Dicks (D-Wash.) responded to the last point. "I, too, was concerned when I was told about the ocean reconnaissance satellites and the possible implications of their use in terms of naval combat or in conventional warfare between our two sides," he said. "I asked the Navy, Vice Admiral Nagler, Director of Command and Control in the Office of Naval Operations, whether the Navy had ways of countering these short of us having an ASAT capability. And he said that they were not overly concerned about this because they had a number of ways of spoofing the RORSAT and the EROSAT satellite that they have. There are a number of ways with electronic countermeasures that they could create false radar signals or make corner reflectors to simulate the radar cross section of a carrier battle group and take other means by which they can handle these low-altitude satellites short of us having an ASAT capability."

Congressman Brown also questioned other aspects of the Byron amendment:

Mr. Brown. There is a problem here that has bothered me about the gentlewoman's amendment and that is . . . we had an operational system based on the THOR missile actually in place and operating for 10 years. We made 22 tests prior to deploying that.

My question is: Do we count the 22 tests for our operational system that we had deployed for 10 years?

Mr. Henry Hyde [(R-Ill.)]. We did not test against an object in space, that was a nuclear system.

Mr. Brown. Yes, we did.

Congressman Samuel S. Stratton (D-N.Y.) interjected to challenge statements about the original U.S. ASAT system. "We have been told that the United States had developed 15 years ago an ASAT system which the Soviets are testing today. This is not true. . . . The old U.S. system was Project 457. It was a booster that was aimed at a particular point in space and was totally different from the current Soviet system, which can actually transfer orbits," he noted. "Those who are supporting the Brown amendment claim that the Soviet ASAT system is a model T. This model T, however, has succeeded 9 out of 15 times."

As the debate drew to a close, Representative Gore summed up the sentiments of many supporters of the Brown amendment. "I believe the administration is wrong on this antisatellite question," he said. "We have here in essence a fail-safe point. If we cross this threshold, then the sky is the limit. . . .

"Why? Because the strategic satellites are perhaps the most stabilizing element in the nuclear arms race today. They give both sides the ability to see and hear what is going on in the other country. We can monitor testing programs. We can see their ICBM sites. We can see when they launch missiles and when they test missiles. And, I might add, we in the United States have a much more elaborate and sophisticated and valuable capacity in space than does the Soviet Union.

"It is to our advantage to have a ban on systems that threaten satellites."

The House approved the Brown amendment by voice vote after first adopting a Gore perfecting amendment by a vote of 238 to 181. The Senate passed its resolution tying ASAT tests to arms control talks three weeks later. The House–Senate compromise became law in October 1984. In addition to requiring the president to seek ASAT talks, the new law limited ASAT tests to three in 1985 and delayed these tests until March 1985.

5

The Senate Continues
The Antisatellite Weapons Debate

On June 12, 1984, the Senate spent most of the day debating ASATs. The vehicle for this debate was an amendment calling upon the president to seek a mutual and verifiable ban or strict limitations on weapons in space and on weapons designed to attack objects in space. The amendment provided that testing and deployment of ASATs would not be allowed unless the president were making a good-faith effort to negotiate with the Soviets to achieve an ASAT limitation or ban. The debate itself covered virtually the entire scope of issues labeled "Star Wars." This chapter presents the highlights of the Senate debate.

Proponents of an ASAT test moratorium wanted to debate the issue as a separate piece of legislation in the form of S.J.Res. 129. But opponents of the resolution were able to block it from reaching the floor, meaning a wait of perhaps a year until it would be considered. For such a time-urgent issue, the delay was too long for the proponents.

The remaining option was to use the Defense Department authorization bill as the vehicle for this resolution. An agreement was reached by Senators Howard Baker (R-Tenn.) and Robert Byrd (D-W. Va.) to allocate June 12, 1984, for debate. This set the stage for a historic Senate session that began at 11:00 a.m. and recessed at 9:07 p.m.[1]

The whole day was spent debating only that issue. The Senate rarely devotes an entire day to floor action on a single amendment. In an extraordinary move, the Senate's doors were closed from 2:00 to 4:38 p.m. in a secret session to review intelligence data. Discussion during this closed session was intense and vigorous, and the classified information convinced many that failure to halt the competition in space weaponry would have grave implications for this nation's security.

The "open" session debate was no less lively or important. Before examining this debate, it is worthwhile to summarize briefly what was accomplished. The Senate first considered the Pressler amendment, which would have prevented the testing or deployment of ASATs unless the president were seeking to negotiate with the Soviet Union on an ASAT ban or restrictions. When debate showed that some senators questioned whether a ban or restrictions would necessarily be in the best interests of the United States, a compromise amendment, introduced by Senator John Warner (R-Va.) and endorsed by Senators Paul Tsongas and Pressler, was proposed. The Pressler amendment then was withdrawn and its backers supported the compromise. Senator Malcolm Wallop (R-Wyo.) later tried to add a new section to the amendment stating that nothing within the amendment should mean that the president was prevented from acting according to his interpretation of the national interest. Essentially, this would have allowed the president to ignore the amendment.

In the end, three votes were taken. The Wallop addition to the compromise amendment failed by a vote of 45 to 48. This was the key vote of the day because Wallop's addition would have gutted the original purpose of the amendment. When it failed, passage of the compromise was ensured.

The second vote, on a motion by Senator Barry Goldwater (R-Ariz.) to table the compromise amendment, failed by a vote of 29 to 65. The final vote on the Warner compromise carried by a vote of 61 to 28.

The debate began with consideration of the original Pressler amendment, which had 33 cosponsors. Senator John Tower (R-Tex.), floor manager of the defense authorization bill, opened the debate by pointing to the "surpassing importance and significance" of the amendment. Pressler then called up his amendment and discussed its purpose and implications. "[This amendment] makes clear that above all else, we must begin immediately to talk to the Soviet Union if we are to avoid a potentially costly and dangerous space arms race.

"I am less concerned about the exact form of a space arms control agreement than about beginning the effort to reach an accord which would keep the space weapons race at the lowest possible, verifiable level. If a total ban on dedicated ASAT weapons is beyond reach, we should try to conclude more limited agreements. A ban on advanced high altitude ASATs is one possibility. But we must negotiate if we are to determine what may and may not be possible in space arms control.

"For this reason, this amendment calls for a ban on dedicated ASATs or, if that is not possible, strict limitations on ASAT, space-based ballistic missile defenses, and other potentially destructive systems and activities in space.

"Second, the amendment provides the President with the option of instituting, as appropriate, a moratorium on ASAT space flight tests during negotiations. Let me emphasize that this amendment leaves this question to the President's discretion. . . .

"Third, the amendment calls for the inclusion of futuristic space-based and space-directed weapons in space arms control talks. The aim here is to reinforce, not renegotiate, the injunctions in the 1972 ABM Treaty. These discussions should help to remove the ambiguities or loopholes that could be exploited by the Soviet Union. For instance, talks could seek to reverse ABM activities such as the current construction of an ABM radar in Krasnoyarsk in Soviet Central Asia.

"Fourth, this amendment provides for the following: . . . It rejects Soviet efforts to constrain the U.S. space shuttle and other peaceful space activities; . . . it calls for increased funding for survivability measures to protect our satellites; and . . . it urges that funds be made available to enhance our monitoring and verification capabilities for space arms control.

"Finally, this amendment requires the submission to Congress of a report detailing the steps taken to open talks with the Soviets on space weaponry since the date of enactment of this legislation.

". . . The United States has a great deal to lose and very little to gain from a space arms race. U.S. interests would be best served if arms control agreements can be reached. In the Senate, as more information becomes available, a growing number of Senators have joined our effort to seek to avert transforming space into another battlefield.

"The strength of support for this amendment is revealing the mood of the Senate today. It is now time for the Senate to endorse a policy of negotiations. This amendment provides a foundation for such Senate action. The Senate must act now. Given the pace of space weapons development, we cannot afford to delay any longer."

Senator Sam Nunn (D-Ga.), ranking minority member of the Senate Armed Services Committee, reviewed the background of the legislation. Nunn noted that the Tsongas amendment, which had passed by a vote of 91 to 0 the previous year, called for a ban, and that the administration responded in March 1984 with a report on ASAT policy. Senator Nunn then gave his impressions of the report. "First, it seems that the Administration's logic is that the Soviets already have an ASAT and we do not. That is partially true, but theirs is not very sophisticated and is easily defeated, in my view.

"Second, the Soviets are also working on lasers to attack our satellites. That is also true, but our satellites can be made much harder and less vulnerable to this threat.

"Third, the Administration says that we could not verify that existing coorbital ASAT or low-power lasers will be removed if banned. That is also true, but in my view, if these are rendered ineffective because of our steps to remove our vulnerability, then it does not really matter if they can be verified because we would no longer be dependent on an arms control treaty to counter those systems that we ourselves counter by rendering our satellites less vulnerable."

Nunn also noted the administration claimed that it was necessary for us to be able to attack Soviet satellites, but he argued that "this is a highly debatable proposition, given the preponderance of studies that have shown the United States' dependence on satellites to be far greater than that of the Soviet Union. . . .

"Unless the Administration is willing to come forth with a program to fix our posture, we are going to remain vulnerable whether or not we have a treaty. That is the point I think should be underscored. . . .

"The final conclusion: Obviously, therefore, the Administration concludes that negotiations with the Soviets at this time would be unpromising. Needless to say, my comment, based on the Administration's propositions, is I think this is a dubious conclusion based on dubious logic."

Senator Nunn rejected the extreme approaches to the issue: one side wanting no testing at all, the other side wanting no arms control. Nunn attacked the House-passed Brown amendment (see Chapter 4) as providing no incentive for the president or the Soviets to pursue arms control in good faith. He concluded by calling for an end to extreme views and stating his belief that ASAT testing can continue simultaneously with an effort to negotiate arms control. "I believe any testing should be carried out with the full view in mind that we hope to have that kind of agreement."

Senator Pete Wilson (R-Calif.) strongly opposed the amendment. "It seeks to require [of] the President of the United States, an action that is ill-advised. . . . It is simply naive to assume that the Soviets would give up this enormous advantage of a tested reliable ASAT capability for the sake of this agreement." Wilson stressed the Soviet threat to U.S. security, noting that the same logic that led them to shoot down a Korean airliner could lead them to take offensive actions against U.S. satellites. He observed that current Soviet technology could shoot down the space shuttle, and that if they advanced farther technologically, they might be tempted to use their technology against some important U.S. satellites.

Senator Charles Percy, chairman of the Senate Foreign Relations Committee, supported the amendment, recalling the ABM debate of the 1960s: "At that time, I was convinced that whatever investment the United States made in strategic defensive weaponry would have been inevitably overtrumped by additional Soviet investments in relatively less expensive offensive systems. The net result would have been that each side would have spent tens of billions of dollars simply to maintain the strategic stalemate at a much higher, more costly and less stable level. . . . I am deeply concerned that the Administration's SDI proposal repeats the error of the original ABM deployment proposal 15 years ago."

Percy called on the United States to "lead the way in trying to negotiate an arms control regime that will, [to] the fullest extent possible, preserve space as a sanctuary from weaponry."

Senator Tower spoke against the amendment, which he called "an exercise in wishful thinking, an exercise in naivete. . . .

"The Soviets are hardnosed negotiators. I do not know where we get the idea that by imposing restraints on our own development and permitting them some superior capability in an area, we are likely to hasten negotiations.". Tower drew on Percy's analogy of ASATs to the ABM treaty, claiming that the Soviets did not negotiate until the United States had authorized, funded, and begun to deploy an ABM system.

At this point, Tower was asked by Senator David Pryor (D-Ark.), "Exactly what area of this sense-of-the-Senate resolution unilaterally ties the hands of the United States of America on this issue?"

Tower responded by reading through the amendment, noting certain parts of it that he believed would tie the hands of the United States. "Why should you have a moratorium during negotiations? It seems to me that during negotiations is the time when you want to be improving your technology so you have something to negotiate with," Tower said. He also observed that verification problems would make it impossible for such a treaty to be concluded: "The fact is, this is a sense-of-the-Congress resolution, but the clear thrust of it is to inhibit, in my view, the negotiating posture of the President. It is, in fact, saying to the world, 'the United States has not been serious about negotiations. Only the Soviets are'.

"Why do we not pass one instead urging the Presidium of the Supreme Soviet to . . . get involved in negotiations. . . .

"The only thing that has been proven is, fund a system, deploy it, and then they will negotiate, and they will conclude a treaty.'"

Tower questioned the "good faith" of Soviet negotiators, saying that the climate created by such a resolution would make it impossible to arrive at a serious agreement with the Soviets. "What was historically shown is we develop and deploy a system and the Soviets negotiate seriously and we limit the system. That is what has been proven to work."

Senator Pryor disagreed with Tower's interpretation. "It would appear to me that this President should not oppose this resolution because it is basically saying in print what he has been saying in public, that he wants to negotiate," Pryor stated. "He is willing to go to the negotiating table. He is willing to talk to the Soviet Union. Here comes the Congress of the United States saying, 'Mr. President, we encourage you to do this. Mr. President, we stand behind you in doing this'."

Pryor also disagreed with Tower's interpretation that the amendment would force a moratorium during negotiations. "The Senator from Texas knows very well on page 1 the Pressler amendment at line 11 [says, institute] 'as appropriate' such a moratorium. 'As appropriate' would certainly give the President of the United States the opportunity to back away from this moratorium if he did not deem it to be appropriate." Pryor added that although he had not known earlier whether or not he would vote for the Pressler amendment, the day's testimony convinced him of a need to send a message to the president to negotiate.

Senator Paul Tsongas observed that there should be no reason to debate another amendment to succeed his 1983 amendment. "The amendment did not demand a signed treaty with the Soviets . . . but it did require at the minimum a Presidential certification that he was willing to make such efforts. That apparently was too much to ask." Tsongas then explained how his 1983 ASAT test ban amendment had been gutted by the Armed Services Committee after the administration report was sent to Congress. "The administration response was, in hindsight, a clever tactical move. They claimed that a ban meant development, testing, deployment and possession. They also said that a ban on ASATs meant everything residual or that could be conceivably used as ASATs, such as space shuttles and ICBMs. Therefore, they argued, they could never satisfy my amendment's requirements—it was too absolute, too comprehensive. . . .

"Well done. If I had been in their predicament, faced with that amendment and feeling no particular enthusiasm for ASAT arms control, I would have done the same thing—seize upon the letter of the law and ignore the spirit. Tactically, a smart move. But the Nation, and I believe the Congress, is not of the same mind. We support a sincere effort to negotiate arms limitations on ASATs."

Tsongas noted that the new amendment did not use the word "ban," but rather "ban or strict limitation." He maintained that the Soviets would be better situated to adapt to unrestrained ASAT competition because they used short-lived satellites that were replaced frequently. "I am convinced that a ban on testing, deployment, and use [of] dedicated ASATs is a negotiable, verifiable proposition. If this administration responds in good faith to this amendment, they will propose to the Soviets a variation on that theme. . . .

"Whether these amendments pass or fail today, there is an obligation on the part of the United States to do something about vulnerability of our satellites. Even those of us who argue for an approach of ASAT arms control would in no way argue with that point.

"What we are going to vote on today is very simple: We are saying to the administration, yes, go ahead with your testing; yes, go ahead with all your R&D; but at least begin to negotiate."

Senator Jeff Bingaman (D-N.M.) spoke in support of the amendment. He stated that people from the Department of Defense were wrong in saying the United States was ten years behind the Soviets in ASAT capability. Most knowledgeable witnesses, according to Bingaman, believe that the U.S. capability is at least equal to the Soviets'.

Bingaman expressed concern that "the administration and some Senators . . . could resist the simple request that the United States be willing to go ahead and endeavor to negotiate." He criticized the administration arguments against ASAT arms control efforts: "The same arguments used to reject ASAT control negotiations could be used to reject arms control negotiations in any area: chemical and biological weapons, strategic weapons, intermediate-range nuclear weapons, conventional forces in Europe, or a comprehensive test ban. In at least the first four of these areas, the administration with varying degrees of enthusiasm has engaged in negotiations."

Bingaman also quoted Assistant Secretary of Defense Richard Perle from March 15, 1984, Senate Armed Services Committee testimony: "Even leaving aside considerations of verifiability, the United States cannot accept arms control limitations that would preclude us from taking action against those satellites in the course of hostilities. . . . What is more, we must acquire as quickly as possible the capability to neutralize such threatening Soviet satellites."

Bingaman asserted, "We cannot deny any adversary the use of space-based systems that provide support to hostile military forces . . . and expect our adversary to do anything but reciprocate by putting our military support satellites at risk."

He also demonstrated that the United States possessed other means to counter Soviet "satellites than to simply shoot them out of the sky." Citing the administration's examples of the potential damage Soviet ocean-reconnaissance satellites could inflict on U.S. naval forces in wartime, Bingaman questioned the danger. He pointed out that such satellites could be made useless through electronic interference, adding that the Soviets possessed other means of targeting opposing naval forces. "Eliminating the satellites," Bingaman claimed, "would only eliminate a fraction of the threat to our naval forces."

The methodology of the administration's study was criticized by Bingaman: "It has struck me in listening to these briefings that we are engaged in the most extreme worst case analysis. The Intelligence Community is taking very speculative information about potential Soviet capabilities, and building them up as a relatively near-term likelihood for purposes of public consumption via selective leaks. . . . The goal is to convince us that the time is past for arms control and stampede us to the conclusion that our choice is to outrace the Soviets in space weaponry."

Senator Bingaman cited the testimony of Dr. Robert Cooper, the head of the Defense Advanced Research Projects Agency, who noted that the intelligence estimates "that we hear and which sound so frightening are estimates based on what the Soviets could possibly do if everything fell into place for them in their development program and if they solved problems we had not yet solved." "In my opinion," said Bingaman, "these intelligence estimates of the Soviet space threat are the basis for only the most paranoid of national policies."

What we must do, according to Senator Bingaman, is determine whether the risks of unconstrained ASAT development outweigh the risks of arms control. He offered examples of the advantages of arms control over a policy of unrestrained development. First, if testing were halted, the Soviets could not develop a more dangerous higher-altitude ASAT. Laser development could be verified, he said, because "lasers produce recognizable signatures when they propagate through the atmosphere and hit targets." The inability of lasers to penetrate clouds means they would be located in regions of the Soviet Union most accessible to overhead inspection. Dr. Michael May of Lawrence Livermore National Laboratory had testified at a Senate Armed Services Committee hearing that "a laser attack to be effective would have to involve high-power lasers and many of them, and at that point the ASAT system becomes detectable and verifiable."

Calling the refusal to negotiate "irresponsible and short-sighted," Bingaman asserted, "We are on the verge of making Mr. Perle's prediction that arms control cannot successfully inhibit technology a self-fulfilling prophecy." A research and development hedge is needed, Senator Bingaman admitted; "but, if the administration will not take the lead in vigorously pressing negotiations to seal off the weaponization of space, leadership by default belongs to the Congress."

Senator Carl Levin (D-Mich.) also spoke in favor of the amendment, summarizing the two outstanding issues involved: Can ASAT testing be verified, and would it be in the national interest to ban the testing of those weapons that could be verified?

On the first issue, Senator Levin noted that both proponents and opponents of a test ban agreed that it could be verifiable. He quoted Richard Perle, as well as OTA. On the second issue, he cited testimony from administration officials that did not rule out the possibility that a limited test ban might be in the national interest. At a committee hearing, Dr. Robert Cooper had been asked if he agreed that limited bans could be within the national interest. He replied, "I would not have agreed to writing the report if I didn't think there was a chance that they might be." Richard Perle also said he would not rule that out forever.

"And so," Senator Levin concluded, "what we have before us are two forms of a resolution, in an amendment, which simply says we should follow two tracks; we should go ahead and test. . . . Let us proceed to do our research and development, but at the same time let us see if we cannot get at least a partial ban on those weapons systems, the testing of which can be verified.

It is a very logical position. It cannot be answered by assertions that it is unilateral or that there is a ban on testing that is unilateral or that we are tying anybody's hands. Nobody's hands are tied."

At this point in the debate, Senator John Warner (R-Va.) offered a compromise amendment that differed from the original Pressler amendment in three respects:

- The compromise amendment did not require negotiations as a precondition for permitting ASAT testing. Rather, the administration would need only to demonstrate that it was endeavoring in good faith to negotiate with the Soviets.

- The compromise added a provision that a test could occur if the president certified that no test would present clear and irrevocable harm to national security.
- The compromise required a more detailed report from the president to Congress.

Although these might appear to be minor, some conservatives who were against the original amendment believed the changes gave the president more leeway. Those who supported the Pressler amendment had no trouble accepting the Warner compromise, and several had participated in developing it. Some felt the compromise was actually stronger than the original amendment: The original amendment said the president "should seek negotiations with the Soviet Union," whereas the compromise amendment said the president "should endeavor in good faith, to negotiate with the Soviet Union." Whether stronger or not, the compromise had the same basic impact as the original amendment: to send a message to the White House that Congress considered ASAT negotiations to be imperative.

Senator Sam Nunn explained what he believed was the most important part of the compromise: "We are requiring the President to submit, with his certification, a report which addresses the vulnerability of our present satellites and also proposes steps to make them less vulnerable.

"It is my view that unless those steps are taken, we really are not ever going to say that an antisatellite treaty is indeed verifiable, and we will continue in the catch-22 position of saying that a treaty is not verifiable, but at the same time not taking the steps necessary to reduce the vulnerability that would allow verifiability as to future threats. I think that is enormously important."

Senator Barry Goldwater (R-Ariz.) was not quite so happy about the compromise. "What are we going to wind up doing—compromise with the Soviet Union across the board? I am not going to vote for this. I think it is a bad piece of legislation."

Senator John Heinz (R-Pa.) took issue with Goldwater and agreed with Nunn that the verification part of the compromise was important. Heinz also echoed Percy's concerns about the ABM treaty: "I am most concerned about antisatellite weapons and their technologics because of their often ignored capability to undermine the Antiballistic Missile Treaty. The relationship of ASAT to boost phase and other missile defense capabilities can quickly lead to the abrogation of the ABM treaty."

Senator Malcolm Wallop (R-Wyo.) spoke out strongly against the compromise amendment. "While it is a compromise and it is perhaps better than where we were, it has gotten us nowhere," he said.

Wallop claimed that the amendment would reward the Soviet Union for staying away from the bargaining table. "Why in heaven's name would anybody expect them to come back for any purpose, if the Senate of the United States and the Congress of the United States continue to provide the negotiating forum within these halls . . . and they give up nothing?"

Wallop also questioned: "Who, may I ask, is to determine what is endeavoring in good faith? Whose determination is that? . . .

"We have provided in this that we cannot do anything, we cannot do any testing unless they agree to a ban, unless there is a clear and irrevocable harm to the country, and that if that clear and irrevocable harm exists, somehow or other, we cannot do anything about it in case it would harm the prospects for a treaty some other place down the road. . . .

"I agree with the Senator from Arizona . . . and I hope that some people look at the language in this amendment and see what it is that we cannot do under it, by law, and see what it is that we have done to reward Chernenko with his curiously comfortably timed announcement that seeks the ban of weapons in space, antisatellite weapons especially, when the Senate is about to begin its debate."

Senator Steve Symms (R-Idaho) also opposed the compromise amendment. "Common sense should be our guide at a time like this. . . . What we have seen is the Soviet Union, with no free press, with no peace demonstrators, with no elections, wait America out. All they have to do is go to the negotiating table and say, no. And pretty soon, the Americans will start negotiating with themselves."

Symms expressed disdain that the United States would weaken its negotiating position. "If I were over in the Kremlin, I would say, if this amendment passes with this great momentum behind it, 'Just stand firm, boys, because the Americans are weakening. They are voting on the Senate floor the same position we would like to see them take to demonstrate that they are weakening their position all the time'."

Symms also reminded his colleagues that the Soviet Union was notorious for violating arms accords, citing testimony by Assistant Secretary of Defense Richard Perle. Perle had claimed that there were "20 to 25 additional cases of Soviet arms control treaty violations under study" beyond those already made public. President Reagan had already made public nine Soviet treaty violations. "Until the Soviets can be made to comply with existing arms control treaties," Symms asserted, "it will be futile to try to negotiate an ASAT arms control treaty."

Senator Strom Thurmond (R-S.C.) also disagreed with the amendment. Reminding the Senate that it was the Soviets who had walked out of the arms control negotiations, Thurmond blamed the intransigence of the Soviet Union for the lack of meaningful arms control talks. "I feel this amendment will unduly restrict President Reagan's ability to conduct negotiations with the Soviet Union," Thurmond claimed. "It is not necessary to legislate the United States into a position of being forced to seek arms control negotiations with the Soviets."

Senator Wallop then submitted the following amendment to the Warner compromise amendment:

AMENDMENT NO. 3187

Add the following to the end of the amendment pending: d) Notwithstanding any provision contained in this section, nothing shall be construed to limit the ability of the President to act in a manner consistent with the national security interests of the United States.

Senator Warner defended the compromise amendment in these words: "I would have to strongly object to the language proffered by the Senator from Wyoming. Similar language was considered as a part of our lengthy negotiations, and it was the considered opinion of almost all in the group who negotiated on this amendment that the effect of such language would render null and void the President's option that is recited prior thereto. For that reason I object to the language. . . .

"The spirit of the Wallop amendment is already present in the language of my amendment. I am concerned, however, that if the Wallop amendment were adopted, a number of Senators who support my amendment would withdraw their support and the Senate would once again be confronted with the amendment of the Senator from South Dakota. I am completely confident that the President will not take any action inconsistent with the national security interest in complying with the requirements of my amendment. Certainly the amendment does not require that he take any such action. . . . It is unnecessary to say that any more clearly than the amendment already does."

Senator Nunn also rejected the new section proposed by Senator Wallop. Nunn stated that such an addition would "cut Congress out of the process completely. If we are going to do that, we could simply put a dollar amount in the defense bill and say the President shall use these dollars consistent with the national security of the United States."

Responding to these arguments, Wallop said: "After all the limits I pointed out in this amendment. . . which give the Soviets a yes or no, go or no go on any testing in the United States simply by not coming to an agreement, we get down to the bottom line of it and the prohibition is open-ended. . . . I cannot believe, despite what they have said, that the leadership of [the] Armed Services Committee . . . would object to a provision that says notwithstanding any provision in this section, nothing shall be construed to limit the ability of the President to act in a manner consistent with the national security interests of the United States."

Senator Joseph Biden, Jr. (D-Del.) disagreed: "The primary purpose of any arms control agreement should be to enhance the U.S. national security. . . . I know how important satellite systems are to our national defense. If even a small fraction of these systems were to be blinded in a crisis, our national command authorities would face extraordinary difficulties assessing and responding to a possible attack. Ignorance and uncertainty would compound our fears and suspicions. No one can be certain what would happen in those terrifying circumstances."

Biden pointed out three ways to protect satellites: (1) improve satellite survivability; (2) seek "mutual agreement on cheatproof provisions to limit" Soviet ASAT systems; and (3) "develop our own weaponry and hope that mutual possession will lead to mutual deterrence against use." Of the first, Biden cited general agreement that it was a good course of action. But he faulted the administration for ignoring the second course in favor of the third. "We may ultimately have to rely on such a [mutual deterrence] policy, but it is reckless not even to try to protect ourselves better by pursuing the first two approaches as far as possible.

"Both the Soviet Union and the United States still have time to forestall this particular space weapons race, for neither nation has a proven system against vital high-altitude satellites. But if we wait, if we let technology go full speed while diplomacy is idling, we may soon find ourselves less secure—just as we did when both sides rushed to develop multiple warhead missiles, which have made the nuclear balance far less stable."

As noted early in this chapter, the Wallop amendment and a Goldwater tabling motion against the compromise Warner amendment were defeated, and the compromise passed, 61 to 28.

The *Washington Post* offered this analysis of the amendment: "The vote was seen more as an effort in prodding the Reagan administration into seeking negotiations with the Soviet Union than as a move to ban space weapons tests, which could go ahead as long as the President meets several conditions, including 'endeavoring' to negotiate 'the strictest possible limitations on antisatellite weapons consistent with national security interests of the United States'."[2]

Within days of the Senate's debate, President Reagan made a declaration welcoming talks with the Soviets. Unfortunately, the Soviet interest in negotiations proved to be less substantial than many hoped. Still, the United States had indicated its willingness to negotiate ASATs, and it was clear that it was the Soviets who were staying away from arms talks.

6

The President Speaks

Tonight . . . I am directing a comprehensive and intensive effort to define a longterm research and development program to begin to achieve our ultimate goal of eliminating the threat posed by strategic nuclear missiles.

President Reagan made this now-famous announcement on March 23, 1983, as he unveiled his landmark SDI[1] in a surprise and dramatic nationwide television address. Technological advances, Mr. Reagan asserted, have made it "reasonable" for the nation's scientists to begin research into BMDs that would protect the United States and its allies from the specter of nuclear holocaust. "I call upon the scientific community who gave us nuclear weapons to turn their great talents to the cause of mankind and world peace: to give us the means of rendering these nuclear weapons impotent and obsolete," he said.

The president's SDI "speech" was actually a last-minute postscript to his address that night about U.S. policy in Central America and the military buildup in Nicaragua. Many top-level officials were taken completely by surprise. The media reported that Secretary of State George Shultz learned about the president's intentions to include strategic defense in the speech only a few days before its delivery. Shultz at the last minute added an assurance that the allies would be included in any defense deployment plan. Dr. Richard DeLauer, then-under-secretary for defense research and engineering at the Pentagon, was said to have learned about the SDI portion of the speech only hours before the president went on nationwide television.

Indeed, testimony before Congress earlier that same day made it clear that most Pentagon officials were "out of the loop" on the new SDI policy. The strategic reason cited in the president's speech for an accelerated research program into developing technologies was the need to catch up with Soviet strategic defense efforts. But just hours before the president's speech, Major General Donald L. Lamberson, director of the Pentagon's Directed Energy Weapons Program, told the Senate Armed Services Committee that the Pentagon did not believe the time had arrived for a crash research program into advanced space weapons-related technology. Lamberson said existing efforts were sufficient to "vigorously address the most critical issues" associated with developing such weapons. He argued against a "Manhattan project-type" effort.[2]

Also on March 23, 1983, Dr. Robert Cooper, the Defense Department's director of advanced research, told the House Appropriations Committee that the United States was spending between $100 and $150 million per year on space-based laser weapons research. He added, "That activity, we believe, is carrying the technology along at a rate which will certainly make it impossible for the Soviets to break out with a capability in space that we could not either duplicate or counter."[3]

Former Secretary of State Alexander M. Haig, Jr., confirmed the Pentagon's dismay beyond any doubt in a speech at the Lawrence Livermore nuclear weapons laboratory in August 1984. Referring to the "ill-timed" Star Wars address, Haig quipped, "I know the aftermath the next day in the Pentagon, where they were all rushing around saying 'What the hell is strategic defense?'"[4]

The president's speech was said to have been inspired in part by his talks with Dr. Edward Teller, the physicist who played a prominent role in developing the hydrogen bomb, and in part by his monthly meetings with the joint chiefs of staff who argued for a reassessment of plans to protect U.S. missile sites. Crucial parts of the speech were written by Dr. George A. Keyworth, the president's science advisor, and Robert C. McFarlane, then-deputy national security advisor—and by the president himself. Other key advisors were certainly consulted as the president moved toward his decision to announce his new, far-reaching program.

A White House press briefing just before the speech made clear that President Reagan envisioned the use of futuristic, directed-energy weapons, such as laser and particle beams, in any new missile defense system. This prompted the media to christen the SDI "Star Wars," after the classic science fiction movie of the same name. And the nickname has prevailed, despite the president's protestations.

Despite its grand introduction, the SDI did not set any new space-age programs into motion. Research was well underway on all the futuristic technological components required for a space-based nuclear shield. Various space-based BMD systems had been proposed earlier and were under study by Congress. The United States was already developing a new and sophisticated ASAT weapon. In September 1982, the U.S. Air Force established a new Space Command. Located beneath Cheyenne Mountain in Colorado, Space Command's function is to manage and control U.S. defense satellites and defense-related space shuttle missions.

What made the president's SDI proposal momentous was that it called for a concerted and accelerated effort, combining all these elements, to create a "total ballistic missile defense." His speech had great emotional appeal. Everyone yearns for a defense system that will protect people from the horrors of nuclear war. But the speech was also extremely controversial, for what Mr. Reagan proposed was potentially the most ambitious and expensive military effort in history. Further, if ultimately deployed, the SDI might upset the 1972 ABM treaty and the strategy of massive nuclear retaliation, the paradox through which the United States and the Soviet Union have maintained an uneasy truce for more than two decades.

One of the first questions raised in congressional debate was whether the president's SDI program would upset the wisdom upon which the ABM treaty was based. Critics said yes. Supporters countered that the doctrine of MAD is immoral and that the ABM treaty prevents the United States from defending its citizens should deterrence ever break down.

SDI proponents also argued that new technologies had reached a level where it was reasonable to consider a change in policy, from mutually assured destruction to mutually assured defense.

As the debate intensified, Congress began to ask expert witnesses more fundamental questions about the future of military planning, strategic doctrine, and arms control considerations. Among other questions raised were these: Will the SDI protect the public or only vulnerable U.S. missiles? Is the technology attainable? Are the costs within the realm of reason? How will our allies react? And, above all, will it reduce or increase the risks of nuclear war?

The remainder of this book considers the role that Congress has taken in response to the introduction of the concept of SDI. The floor debates of the Senate and the House, the purpose of the various pieces of legislation introduced there, especially those related to funding the SDI program, and the hearings held by House and Senate committees are the subjects of Chapter 7. The remaining chapters address in detail key issues of the SDI—its relation to the

ABM treaty, comparisons of U.S. and Soviet space system costs and technology, strategic implications, and the impact on the European allies. Many of the later chapters use other congressional sources of information, for example, reports required of the executive branch or one of the arms of Congress, such as OTA.

The president's address focused national attention on weapons in space. To be sure, Congress had already devoted some time to the subject. The first part of the book has addressed the ASAT aspects of the subject. Congress had also held hearings on the High Frontier proposals of former Director of the Defense Intelligence Agency General Daniel O. Graham. The High Frontier concept advocates an ABM defense using technology currently available. The remainder of this book examines Congress's often frustrating efforts to understand the strategic implications of the SDI, reactions of our NATO allies and the Soviet Union, the effect of the SDI on international treaties, and its technology.

7

Congressional Actions on the Strategic Defense Initiative

Congress, for the most part, was caught off guard by the remarks of the president. Several Democratic members of the House responded the following day with sharp criticism of the SDI concept.

Congressman Les AuCoin (D-Ore.) found "the President's views simplistic and dangerously out of step with the people of my district. And I have regrettably come to the conclusion that this President is not content with deterrence. He wants instead military superiority." AuCoin called for a "nuclear weapons freeze which stops this 'Dr. Strangelove' insanity, and allows the energies of our scientists to be put not to the militarization of space, but rather to economic technology, the reduction of hunger, and disease, and ignorance, and the creation of jobs for Americans here at home."[1]

Congressman Howard Wolpe (D-Mich.) declared, "Last night the American people were treated to one of the most outrageous and misleading pieces of political propaganda that this Nation has seen in many years." The defense budget, Mr. Wolpe asserted, was already bloated and wasteful.

"Never in my wildest dreams could I ever imagine," Congressman Ted Weiss (D-N.Y.) asserted, "our President taking to the national airwaves to promote a strategy of futuristic 'Star Wars' schemes as Mr. Reagan did last night. . . . Clearly, Mr. Reagan seeks to elevate the current nuclear madness to a new dimension."

Congressman Jim Moody (D-Wis.) stated that "the President is asking our Nation to embark on a highly technical, problematic, and expensive weapon system. This runs directly counter to the majority of Americans who support cuts in our Defense budget, particularly in the area of exotic weapons procurement."

Congressman Thomas J. Downey (D-N.Y.) remarked that "the only thing the President did not tell us last night was the Evil Empire was about to launch the Death Star against the United States." He went on to say "that the . . . second part of his speech, . . . where he talks about a future ABM system in outer space, is probably the most appalling and ridiculous idea that he offered last night."

Congressman Edward J. Markey (D-Mass.) explained that, to the president, "the Force of Evil are the Soviets. They are Darth Vader. We are Luke Skywalker and we are the Force of Good." Edward Teller, the original E.T., Mr. Markey asserted, must not be allowed to lead us into "some kind of pinball outer space war between the 'Force of Evil and the Force of Good'."

The following week, Congressman Jim Leach (R-Ia.) questioned the soundness of the president's proposal, and encouraged the administration to pursue arms control negotiations with the Soviets.[2] Other than a few occasional remarks, there was no further discussion of the SDI on the floor of the House during the remainder of 1983. However, additional debate did occur in committee in respect to H.R. 3073, the People Protection Act, introduced by Congressman Ken Kramer (R-Colo.).

Congressman Kramer's bill was introduced on May 19, 1983, and was followed on November 10, 1983, with a hearing before the House Armed Services Subcommittee on Research and Development as well as the Armed Services Subcommittee on Investigations. The bill endorsed a proposal to shift U.S. strategic policy to one that would "seek to save lives in time of war, rather than to avenge them," called for a reorganization and consolidation of U.S. directed-energy research and military space activities, and encouraged an assessment of various aspects of strategic defenses and arms control treaties.

During the hearing, Congressman Kramer characterized President Reagan's SDI proposal as "a call for a 'Peace Race' " and "a colossal 'Manhattan Project for Peace'."[3] He indicated that his People Protection Act would help to accomplish the president's objectives through the following changes.

"One, restructure the Air Force Space Command as an all-service unified command that ultimately would have full responsibility for the deployment and operation of all space-defense systems.

"Two, create a new Army command, as a component of the unified space command, which would be responsible for the ground-based aspects of a comprehensive multitiered strategic defense.

"Three, establish a directed energy weapons systems agency to consolidate our research and development work on laser, particle-beam, microwave, and other promising technologies.

"Four, transfer to the Department of Defense those space shuttles which are required for national security missions.

"Five, provide for the immediate development of a manned space station, and

"Six, overhaul our strategic and arms control policies to place primary emphasis on strategic defense rather than strategic offense.

"I am very pleased to learn that many of the recommendations of the defensive technology study team, which has come to be known as the Fletcher Commission, the future security strategy group and the senior interagency group on defense policy reportedly closely parallel the major provisions of the People Protection Act."[4]

Congressman Kramer argued that the functional reorganization and consolidation proposed in his bill would produce a research and operational structure more responsive to the president. He recommended establishing a unified space command based on the existing Air Force Space Command in Colorado Springs and the Naval Space Command. Kramer offered the following rationale for proceeding with the shift from a strategic offensive policy to a strategic defensive posture: "In conclusion, I believe that mutual assured destruction is a morally bankrupt philosophy that places Government in the untenable position of refusing to defend its citizenry. What the President has proposed is no less than a moral recovery in American strategic policy which would take us from the horror of MAD to the promise of mutual assured protection. It is a goal which deserves the fervent support of all who yearn for a world safe from nuclear weapons. Unless we are willing to accept the prospect of a nuclear Pearl Harbor from space, we must now join the President in a new national commitment to mutual assured protection."[5]

A majority of the other 15 witnesses at this hearing, including Dr. Edward Teller, Dr. Colin Gray, General Daniel Graham, and former astronaut Buzz Aldrin, supported the basic direction of the People Protection Act. For example, Dr. Gray, a member of the General Advisory Commission on Arms Control, said, "Strategic defense constitutes largely unknown territory in both policy and technical terms. The People Protection Act of 1983 serves a vitally useful function in providing both proposals supportive of the President's initiative of March 23, and a focus for constructive discussion. The potential benefits of strategic defense are so significant for the question of peace or war that I hope, though with only modest expectations, that we can proceed with open minds to see if the journey truly will be worth the effort required. On matters of Government organization, the People Protection Act effectively challenges the executive branch to commit itself in management reality to the public policy that it says is authoritative."[6]

Among the opponents were representatives of pro-arms control groups, including Professor Hans Bethe of Cornell University and the Union of Concerned Scientists, whose written statement to the subcommittee concluded: "If it is really our objective to reduce the exposure of our population to nuclear weapons, we must avoid a commitment to global BMD, for that will produce precisely the opposite result: a large expansion of nuclear forces aimed against us, combined with a vastly complex defensive system whose performance will remain a deep mystery until the tragic moment when it will be called into action. It is difficult to imagine a more unstable and hazardous confrontation. And it is also puzzling why anyone should believe that that is the road to a less dangerous world, for a direct, cheap, and safe road is known to exist: negotiated and verifiable deep, deep cuts in strategic offensive forces, and non-nuclear alternatives to our excessive reliance on nuclear weapons."[7]

Congressional interest in the SDI intensified during the second session of the Ninety-Eighth Congress. Hearings before the Senate and House Armed Services Committees and the Appropriations Subcommittees took up the issue of funding for SDI research.[8] Debate on the defense authorization bills in both houses developed into sharp exchanges on various aspects of the SDI. The House Committee on Foreign Affairs held a series of four hearings on weapons in outer space during the year,[9] and the Senate Foreign Relations Committee held two.[10] Subjects discussed at the hearings included ASATs, the SDI, and other space issues.

Discussion of the SDI on the floor of the House in 1984 was limited. When discussing Congressman George Brown's ASAT amendment to the defense authorization bill, members sometimes strayed into the gray area separating the research aspects of ASAT from those of the SDI.[11] The author of the amendment reminded his colleagues of the distinction.[12]

Debate on the Senate floor centered on an amendment by Senator Charles Percy (R-Ill.) to cut $100 million from the SDI research program in the Department of Defense Authorization Act for Fiscal Year 1985. In introducing his amendment, Senator Percy stressed: "This amendment does not kill the SDI. The amendment still provides $1.527 billion for research and development of SDI-related technologies. According to estimates prepared by the Congressional Budget Office, this figure represents over a 50-percent increase in R&D for SDI-related programs over the level provided for the same programs in fiscal year 1984. This increase in SDI funding, I might add, is more than double the requested 26 percent increase for all defense R&D programs. . . .

"The [$100 million] difference . . . may seem small to some. But I would stress that the fiscal year 1985 SDI request is just the tip of the iceberg. We know that the Pentagon intends to request $3.8 billion for the SDI next year, and that the total 5-year costs may approach $26 billion. None of this money—not a penny—will buy a single missile, gun, tank or submarine. . . .

"This amendment . . . is a deficit-reduction amendment. It is a vote for fiscal responsibility. It is not a referendum on 'Star Wars'."[13]

Speaking in support of the amendment, Senator William Proxmire (D-Wis.) warned that the SDI program would "plunge this Nation ahead on a spending binge that will, if we follow through with it, cost our Federal Government a trillion dollars or more." He also questioned the wisdom of the overall strategy of the SDI.[14]

In rebuttal, Senators John Tower (R-Tex.) and Barry Goldwater (R-Ariz.), as well as others, defended the necessity of a research program. In all, more than a dozen senators spoke at length during the debate. By a vote of 47 to 45, the amendment was defeated. The final sum of $1.4 billion was authorized for SDI research in fiscal year 1985 by a conference agreement adopted by the House and Senate later in the year.

Another amendment introduced on June 13 by Senator Pressler was less controversial. The Senate gave voice vote approval to the amendment, which required the Department of Defense to provide Congress with annual reports containing detailed information clarifying SDI objectives. The first annual report reached Congress in April 1985.

Pressler also presented a Congressional Budget Office study on the SDI that documented the necessity of clarifying which Department of Defense and Department of Energy programs were related to the SDI program but not budgeted as part of it.[15]

On June 19, 1984, Senator Proxmire, who spoke frequently against the SDI on the Senate floor in 1985, offered another noncontroversial amendment.[16] It expressed the sense of Congress "that the President shall inform and make every effort to consult with" our NATO allies, Japan, and other appropriate allies concerning SDI research. The amendment required the Departments of State and Defense, as well as ACDA, to report to Congress each year on the status of those consultations. The Senate accepted the amendment without debate.

A concurrent resolution was introduced in October 1984 by Senator John Chafee (R-R.I.) to encourage the president to comply with the ABM treaty.[17] This was the last legislative effort on the SDI in the Senate during 1984. The Committee on Foreign Relations took no action on the resolution.

On April 4, 1985, the Senate Armed Services Committee reported to the full Senate S. 1029, the fiscal year 1986 defense authorization bill providing $3.42 billion for SDI research programs. The committee report[18] indicated that this amount was $300 million below the administration's budget request because of budgetary constraints. It expressed support for the strategic defense concept, concern for the Soviet Union's expanding BMD capability as well as the growing arsenal of Soviet missiles aimed at Western Europe, and encouragement of continued U.S. consultation with the allies.

By the time floor debate began on the defense bill on May 17, the Senate had approved a fiscal year 1986 budget resolution providing $9.1 billion less budget authority for national defense than the Armed Services Committee had assumed in S. 1029. This necessitated reducing many programs and the reporting of a new defense authorization bill, S. 1160. The new recommended amount for the SDI, the amount that was the focus of several amendments on the floor, was $2.97 billion.[19] As with the previous defense bill, it was the committee's position that the SDI funding reduction, now $750 million below the administration's original request, was the result only of budgetary constraints.

When the Senate debated authorizations for ASAT and SDI research funding in May and June 1985, the mood in the Senate concerning space weaponry had been altered by a new development. Foremost was the return of the Soviets to the negotiating table in Geneva. It was widely believed that Soviet apprehension about the SDI had been a major factor in the renewed desire to negotiate. Many senators felt a responsibility not to undercut U.S. negotiators by voting to cut funding for programs that could be used as "bargaining chips" in Geneva. It was in this general atmosphere that debate took place during consideration of the Department of Defense authorization bill for fiscal year 1986.

On May 24, 1985, Senator John Kerry (D-Mass.) offered an amendment calling for a moratorium on ASAT testing.[20] Unlike the existing test limitation, which allowed a maximum of three tests if the president made a number of certifications to Congress, the Kerry amendment proposed to allow ASAT testing only if the Soviets tested an ASAT of their own against an object in space. The amendment also would have permitted continued tests by the United States against points, but not objects, in space. This, Kerry argued, would give flexibility for research with the option to test if the Soviets went ahead with their program.

Kerry reiterated many of the arguments that had been made previously about ASAT testing. He noted that the Soviets' ASAT capability was poor—they could not damage important military satellites with weaponry already tested. Kerry argued that a U.S. test would lead to an unlimited arms race in ASAT weaponry. He said this would be bad for the United States, which relies on satellite information more than the Soviets. Noting that the Soviet Union was observing a "voluntary" moratorium on ASAT testing, Kerry argued that "to preserve the Soviet moratorium, all the United States needs to do is to act with reciprocal restraint."

A letter sent to all senators by Kenneth L. Adelman, director of ACDA, claimed that the United States was not observing a moratorium at this time and planned tests only for technical reasons. This, Kerry stated, showed blatant disregard of the 1983 law that required the president to certify that (1) the United States was endeavoring in good faith to negotiate with the Soviet Union for a mutual, verifiable agreement on ASAT weapons, (2) the ASAT test was necessary to avert irrevocable harm to national security, (3) such testing would not be an irreversible step that would gravely impair prospects for ASAT negotiations, and (4) such testing would be fully consistent with the ABM treaty. Kerry argued that Adelman's letter proved the need for tougher standards to limit ASAT testing.

Senators John Warner (R-Va.) and Sam Nunn (D-Ga.) both spoke against the Kerry amendment, while expressing disappointment in the Adelman letter. "I take the provision now in the law very seriously," Senator Nunn stated, "and would emphasize that before the first test of the U.S. ASAT against an object in space can be conducted, the President must certify that the United States is endeavoring in good faith to negotiate the strictest possible ASAT limitations."

Senator Goldwater said the amendment would "call for the United States to accept one of the Soviet conditions for negotiation. . . . I do not think the U.S. Senate wants to be in the position of offering our enemy an advantage over us."

Senator Pressler expressed reluctant opposition to the amendment: "The circumstances we are operating under in May of 1985 are different from the ones we operated under in November 1983. The Congress should not try to micromanage diplomacy and defense by binding every defense development to some diplomatic contingency."

Senator John Chafee (R-R.I.) supported the Kerry amendment. Chafee argued that the Soviets could match the United States if the latter were to test sophisticated ASATs. Such a development would pose a greater threat to the United States because of its greater reliance on satellites, he said. Chafee, emphasizing that the amendment would permit the president to order tests if the Soviets started testing again, claimed that there was no real reason to oppose the amendment.

Senator Jeff Bingaman (D-N.M.) pointed out that the previous ASAT legislation had a limit of three tests, which was designed as an incentive for both sides to negotiate. The Soviets would negotiate because they would want to prevent the development of a superior U.S. ASAT, and U.S. interests would be served by arms talks because three tests would not be enough to ensure reliable deployment of its ASAT. Bingaman questioned the deletion of the three-test limitation provision from the Kerry amendment.

Senator Kerry replied that many had accepted the three-test limit because they knew the United States could not complete three tests at that time. He argued that it would be wrong to start testing at a time when both sides were at the negotiating table and when the Soviets were observing a self-imposed moratorium.

Senator Warner responded to a similar question by stating that he would be offering an alternative amendment to the Kerry amendment, which would provide restraints on ASAT testing similar to the previous law.

Kerry concluded the case for his amendment by claiming that it "in no way gives something unilaterally to the Soviet Union. . . . We always seem to fall prey to that argument: One more time, give us one more system, give us one more piece, give us another satellite, give us another ship, give us another missile, give us one more . . . and there is not one bargaining chip in history that has even made that kind of difference. We just go on to the next level of building."

After the amendment failed by a vote of 35 to 51, Senator Warner offered an amendment to limit ASAT testing to three tests. The president would be required to make the certifications called for in the 1983 law in order to exceed that limit.

Senator Bingaman said he was troubled by the fact that if the president made the required certification, he could test as many

ASATs as he wanted. "My concern about this amendment," he said, "is that it takes the limits off, or takes the restrictions off, the number of tests the administration can conduct in 1986 so that if any ambitious testing schedule were pursued, our ASAT system could become fully operational within fiscal year 1986, which I think also is contrary to what we intended last year."

Agreeing that there was no limit on the number of permissible ASAT tests under the amendment, Senator Warner insisted that the effect would not be contrary to the intent of Congress. Warner pointed out that the Congress would still have the chance to rescind the use of funds after presidential certification, thereby curtailing any test program. Senator Nunn emphasized that the amendment required the president not only to certify the need for the first three tests, but also to recertify the necessity for further tests if more than three tests were desired. Senator Kerry indicated he would support the Warner compromise, although he wanted stronger provisions. With very little debate, the Warner compromise was adopted by a vote of 74 to 9.

On June 3 and 4, the Senate took up fiscal year 1986 defense authorization bill amendments that dealt with the SDI. On June 3, Senator Kerry introduced an amendment to freeze SDI funding at $1.4 billion. The amendment also would eliminate parts of the SDI program that might run afoul of the ABM treaty.[21]

The arguments in favor of the freeze were familiar. Kerry argued that is easier to attack than to defend in the nuclear era and that "the Soviet Union would turn its resources into improving or replacing a portion of its weapons to sidestep the defense." He also pointed out that not all attacking weapons could be stopped by a strategic defense and therefore population centers could not be completely protected. Methods of delivering nuclear weapons other than by land-based missile would not be affected by an SDI-type system. Kerry quoted Soviet dissident Andrei Sakharov who said in 1967: "Under the present political and technological conditions, a 'shield' could create the illusion of invulnerability. For the 'hawks' and the 'madmen', a shield would increase the lure of nuclear blackmail. It would strengthen their attraction to the idea of a preventive thermonuclear strike."

In supporting the amendment, Senator William Proxmire (D-Wis.) said, "At $1.4 billion, we will still have a massive research program, one of the biggest we have ever had." Senator Paul Simon (D-Ill.) added his support for the measure, noting that cost estimates of a deployed system ranged from $126 billion to $1.3 trillion. "The Interstate Highway System has cost us $123 billion. You are talking about something that is going to cost many times more than the Interstate Highway System. How do we pay for it?" he asked.

Kerry spoke again on behalf of his amendment, adding that it was a mistake for the administration to condemn the Soviet radar system near Krasnoyarsk as a violation of the ABM treaty, when the SDI constituted preparation for the United States to violate it. He concluded that the SDI would be useless in the long run anyway: "Even if we spend these trillions of dollars, even if we develop a star wars system as the best expert can define it, even if that system can knock down 90 percent of the weapons the Soviet Union were to send at us, we still would be left in exactly the same predicament then as we are today, which is making judgments about how badly they can hit us and how badly we can hit them, and we would still be living under the cloud of mutual assured destruction."

Senator Goldwater disagreed. "I do not look upon the SDI exactly as my friend from Massachusetts looks at it. I look upon it as an antiweapon. . . . For every weapons system that has been developed, there has been an antiweapons system developed against it, and they are always successful," he said. Goldwater argued that throughout history, no weapon had been the final word in waging war. Time and technology would make it possible to produce an antiweapon to nuclear weapons, and it would be a mistake not to try to develop it. He asserted, "There is no end . . . to what this country can do if it makes up its mind to do it," and compared the SDI debate to the 1960s' debate on putting a human on the moon before 1970, despite doubts that this could be accomplished. Goldwater predicted, "I think we can perfect one that will shoot down any missile that is fired in our direction."

Under questioning from Senator Dale Bumpers (D-Ark.), Senator Nunn admitted that there were many aspects of the SDI program with which he was uncomfortable, and that the Senate was not yet sure exactly what the program entailed; nonetheless, he felt further research with expanded funding was necessary.

When debate on the SDI funding freeze amendment resumed on June 4, Senator Goldwater pointed out that the Soviets had increased their armaments and already had violated the ABM treaty with the Krasnoyarsk radar system.[22] He felt Senator Kerry had understated Soviet military actions that conflicted with treaty restraints.

Kerry agreed that the Soviets were active in these areas. The point was not what the Soviets could do or were doing, he argued, but whether the SDI itself was worth funding at a higher level. Kerry stated his amendment would not cut SDI research, and would even permit an increase in certain types of research. He reiterated the point that the Soviets could overwhelm U.S. defenses by increasing offensive missile production. "Every single major arms expert in this nation has said the Soviet Union will respond by building offensive weapons to overwhelm our defense. It just happens to be that no scientists in this country . . . assert that it can be 100 percent effective. It cannot be 100 percent effective."

Senator James Exon (D-Neb.) spoke against the Kerry amendment, noting that he had recently been in Geneva and had talked with U.S. negotiators there. "I am convinced more than ever that we will have to use every possible tool and incentive we have in order to make progress and hopefully to obtain a workable and verifiable agreement. SDI in this concept is the best tool we have available and the amount proposed in the amendment before us would, in my opinion, make the tool less effective," he said. Exon indicated that the president had requested $3.7 billion for the SDI and that the request had already been reduced by the Armed Services Committee to $2.97 billion.

Senator Edward Kennedy (D-Mass.), in supporting the amendment, pointed out that it would fund some important research at an increased level. "The amendment would actually increase basic research by 23 percent, by transferring funds away from costly, public relations demonstrations which threaten the ABM Treaty, into more valuable treaty compliant research."

Senator Warner disagreed: "In my judgment this amendment would simply gut the SDI program. It would leave it in a shape that would question whether we should go forward with it in any way." Warner also said the amendment was riddled with technical errors that would be unwise to accept. Finally, he claimed that Senate Armed Services Committee hearings had concluded that the proposed program of SDI research was in full compliance with every term of the ABM treaty.

After the Kerry amendment was defeated by a vote of 21 to 78, Senator Proxmire offered an alternative amendment to fund SDI at a level of $1.9 billion. The amendment provided that the difference between that figure and the $2.97 billion level recommended by the committee would be used for military readiness accounts, such as ammunition and spare parts. Senator Proxmire inserted into the record letters from three former secretaries of defense—Robert McNamara, Clark Clifford, and Elliot Richardson—all stating that a $1.9 billion funding level would be adequate for the SDI in fiscal year 1986. Proxmire gave four major reasons supporting a lower funding level for the SDI: "First, we may be pumping hundreds of millions of dollars into space demonstration projects that may not have any military value later when we learn about other technologies. . . . Second, the problem with rushing into demonstration projects is that they tend to freeze the technology being demonstrated before it is fully mature. . . . Third, technology demonstration projects tend to absorb money from other research projects. . . . And fourth, the technology demonstrations SDI plans seem headed towards violations of the ABM Treaty." The amendment also would have established a Threat Analysis Program, funded at $20 million in fiscal year 1986.

Senator Charles Mathias (R-Md.), a cosponsor of the amendment, agreed that a vigorous research program was needed, but felt that "the SDI must be crafted in such a way as to permit the most cost-effective allocation of resources." He considered the proposed 33 percent funding increase from the previous year to be adequate. Mathias also expressed concern about the impact of the SDI on the NATO alliance. "A national leader in one of the NATO nations," Mathias reported, "told me recently that the presentation of star wars in Europe was a 'disaster' for the United States and for NATO. And he further called it a 'gift to Soviet propaganda'. Those words of warning come from a proven friend of America." Mathias added that France, Norway, and Denmark already had announced their intention not to participate in the SDI projects. He also cited reports that stated that the SDI could "cause serious divisions in the Western alliance."

Senator Warner disagreed, citing the need of U.S. negotiators to have SDI as a bargaining chip. Mathias admitted that Warner had a point, but he said that negotiations could be harmed even more if the SDI were to divide NATO: "What will happen to our negotiators in Geneva when the vibrations coming from Paris, from Copenhagen, from Oslo, from Bonn—yes, from Bonn—begin to indicate that the pressures which star wars is placing on the allied governments are destabilizing the political systems in those countries?"

Senator Pete Wilson (R-Calif.) spoke against the Proxmire amendment. Wilson reiterated the claim that the Soviets had returned to the negotiating table because of the SDI. "And in a fit of rare candor," Wilson said, "the Soviet Union has made abundantly clear that the reason they are back at the tables at all in Geneva far earlier than anyone had thought possible and having abandoned all their stated preconditions to return is because of their clear concern about the strategic defense initiative." Wilson urged continued support of SDI funding, holding out for a possible arms control agreement that might lead to "radical reductions in Soviet offensive weaponry."

Senator Bumpers, also a cosponsor of the amendment, spoke vigorously in favor of it. Noting "optimistic" projections that the SDI could destroy only 90 percent of incoming missiles and that the Soviet Union could increase its nuclear arsenal to 35,000 warheads by 1995, he pointed out that 3,500 missiles would still hit the United States. He added that the Soviets could use inexpensive decoys, all of which would have to be detected or destroyed.

Bumpers also raised the response time factor, claiming the Soviets could reduce their missile boost phase from five to two and one-half minutes, and perhaps less. "Is the world safer," Bumpers asked, "when the time for the President to trigger the SDI and start destroying everything that looks like a boost [is cut] to two and one-half minutes from five minutes?"

Senator Bennett Johnston (D-La.) expressed the concern that the billions of dollars for SDI might be wasted. "There has been no breakthrough. There has been no discovery. We are not on the threshold of building a new weapons system," Johnston claimed. He said the SDI program was based on a speech by President Reagan "which was wrong," and asserted that nobody who had studied the issue could agree that the program would make nuclear weapons obsolete. "We are doing this little dance tonight because the political landscape has been changed by a speech we all know to be wrong," Johnston declared. "Can it ever make nuclear weapons obsolete? Mr. President, even if you had a leak-proof system it would not make nuclear weapons obsolete. . . . The Russians can put these nuclear weapons in a pouch, and the pouch . . . can be a great big van or something. . . . They send in big vans of material all the time. They can put nuclear weapons . . . in a truck, drive it down by Lafayette Park, and have it wait there until the appropriate moment when somebody pushes a button. They can have those all over the country." Johnston also said, "We do not know whether we would want to build it to violate the treaty and we do not know what it would cost, we do [not] know what it would do. The only thing we are sure of is that the President is wrong, that it cannot make nuclear weapons obsolete."

Senator Nunn, while opposing the Proxmire amendment, agreed that Senator Johnston had a good point: "We can certainly agree that the definition as given by the President is not something that can be taken seriously by people who have studied this. . . . The definition as given by Paul Nitze is something different. The definition given by Secretary Weinberger is something different again. The definition given by General Abrahamson is something different again. So which definition are we going to choose? I think the Senate has to follow

that along and see where we come out and see what we agree upon."
He also said, "I can support parts of this amendment, but I cannot
support a detailed micromanagement approach when, as the
Senator from Louisiana articulated so clearly this evening, we have
not even a definition of where we want to go."

Senator Johnston concluded his statement with these remarks:
"I can tell you that former Secretary Jim Schlesinger told us in our
briefing the other day that the word is out on the street that they are
looking for good scientists to come on board, and they will fund
them nicely and send them to Europe, have them talk to Europeans.
This is what former Secretary Schlesinger said is really going on.

"So that would kind of co-opt the whole scientific community.
You make them all part of it. When you have this kind of money to
spread around, you can make little grants. I do not mean to say you
buy the integrity of the scientists, but you get them on board, working for it, and they believe in the program. That is human nature. We
all feel like that.

"You get in one political party, and you tend most of the time to
believe what comes out. At least, if somebody is paying your freight,
you tend to believe that.

"I am very much afraid that what is going to happen with SDI
for the scientific community, and later the Senate, is what happened
on the B-1 bomber. I sat in the Senate, as other Senators did, and
saw Senator after Senator vote the interests of his State.

"That is what I am afraid, in part, is going to happen with SDI,
because it involves so many dollars. We build this whole air castle
out of a speech nobody believes. We purchase all the minds in the
country, in support of it, and pretty soon we in the Senate are
rushing out chasing the tail of that SDI, not knowing where we are
going, but ending up with a country that is closer to bankruptcy
than it is now—and some say it is pretty close—and certainly no
more secure than it is now."

Senator Strom Thurmond (R-S.C.), in opposing the amendment,
discussed its impact on several research programs: "While the amendment's sponsors argue that they are preserving near-term deployment
options involving conventional defensive technologies, their amendment in fact decimates these programs." He identified cuts in the airborne optical adjunct program, the terminal imaging radar program,
and others, noting the conventional uses these programs would have.

Senator Pressler also opposed the amendment, citing recent
discussions with NATO leaders. He mentioned German Foreign
Minister Hans-Dietrich Genscher's belief that the SDI program had
brought the Soviets back to negotiations in Geneva.

The Proxmire amendment was defeated by a vote of 38 to 57, making it the closest vote on any of the amendments to cut SDI funding.

Senator Albert Gore (D-Tenn.) offered an amendment designed to fund the SDI at $2.5 billion, while imposing restrictions on certain projects that might lead to ABM treaty violations. These projects would receive limited funding until the president reported on the need and purpose for the programs and their consistency with the ABM treaty, and until Congress adopted a resolution releasing additional funds. Gore noted that the $2.5 billion mark was an 80 percent increase over the previous year's funding level and explained that he had chosen that level "plainly and simply on the basis that it is very likely the lowest number that the Senate might choose to legislate." He defended the micromanagement provisions of the amendment, arguing that certain programs would lead to ABM violations in the future. Gore said the Senate needed to act now to preserve the meaning of the ABM treaty.

Senator Paul Simon (D-Ill.) agreed. He argued that the United States must create a better climate for arms control and that research leading to ABM violations does not contribute to such an effort.

Senator Warner pointed out that the committee bill already contained provisions against actions that could violate the ABM treaty. He quoted from the bill: "Action by the Congress [in] approving funds for research on the Strategic Defense Initiative does not express or imply an intention on the part of Congress that the United States should abrogate, violate or otherwise erode such treaty, and does not express or imply any determination or commitment on the part of Congress that the United States deploy ballistic missile strategic defense weaponry that would contravene such treaty." "So we have put in here the restriction the Senator from Tennessee essentially desires," Warner stated. "It is in the bill now." The Gore amendment failed by a vote of 36 to 59.

Following the Gore amendment, Senator John Glenn (D-Ohio) made a final attempt to cut SDI funding to $2.8 billion, with no micromanagement provisions. He explained his choice of $2.8 billion: "I see a need for $2.8 billion based on several factors, not just that it is double this year's budget for star wars, but also because General Abrahamson says he has committed $2.2 billion to $2.5 billion in fiscal year 1986 money in existing projects. Now, this means at $2.8 billion we can fund current research and still give him enough extra flex money of $300 to $400 million."

Senator Warner advised that the House Armed Services Committee had authorized $2.47 billion, $500 million less than the amount the Senate was considering: "We need the higher amount in order to negotiate in that conference. So, I ask my distinguished colleague, in view of the need to get $2.8 billion and the present difference of $500 million with the House, would it not be wiser to let the mark, as established in the bill, remain tonight and the Senator join us in the conference to see whether or not we can hold that figure of $2.8 billion and hopefully some more?"

Debate on the Glenn amendment was brief, and the amendment failed by a 36 to 59 margin.

Senator Bumpers then offered an amendment to set up an independent panel to study the SDI. He explained: "It simply sets up a panel of 8 persons to be appointed by the Speaker of the House and the minority leader and by the majority leader and the minority leader of this body. The intent is very simple. It is designed to have somebody look at this program, how the money is being spent, and report back to Congress."

Senator Goldwater complained that the panel would duplicate efforts by the General Accounting Office, OTA, and the Committee on Armed Services, which he chaired. Senators Warner and Nunn persuaded Bumpers to temporarily lay aside the amendment in order to develop a compromise with the Committee on Armed Services. Bumpers then withdrew his amendment.

The next amendment was offered by Senator Malcolm Wallop (R-Wyo.). It specified that $800 million of the total for the SDI should be earmarked for the development of defense systems against ballistic missiles that could be deployed within five to seven years. Wallop said, "The strategic defense initiative as it is right now would not spend a single penny to build any device or any components of any device that would shoot down a missile. . . . And so this amendment goes against the grain of today's Pentagon, and against the grain of what this body has done in the field of strategic weapons. This amendment proposes, strange to say, that we use a little of the money we spend to actually give something useful to ourselves." Wallop criticized Pentagon and congressional management of the SDI and other military projects. "The question is," he said, "do we build weapons, or not?" Notwithstanding his explanation, Wallop's amendment failed by a vote of 33 to 62.

Senator Bumpers then reoffered his amendment setting up a strategic defense advisory panel. The original amendment had been altered to create a ten-member panel, appointed by the ranking majority and minority members of the Senate Armed Services Committee, the Senate Foreign Relations Committee, and the majority and minority leaders of the Senate. Senator Levin, a cosponsor of the amendment, noted that the amendment was a result of work with Senators Goldwater, Nunn, and Warner.

Senator Wilson, however, opposed the amendment, arguing that the panel would still duplicate efforts by OTA, the General Accounting Office, and the Senate Armed Services Committee. "It simply is one more layer, and I think we have all at one time or another agreed with various articles, various programs that have criticized Congress for endless overlay upon overlay . . . a confusing and delaying factor that impedes the work of Congress rather than supports it." He complained that the panel might "set up one quintessential screening panel that may very well supplant needed expert advice that is otherwise available to us from a variety of sources."

Senator Nunn disagreed, pointing to a number of panels and commissions that had advised Congress on various weapons systems and other issues. Nunn noted that the complexity of the SDI would make a special panel to advise the Congress potentially helpful. "So I am not saying this panel is going to solve all the problems, but I certainly do not believe it is going to create any problems that do not already exist," he said.

Senator Goldwater, although he accepted the amendment (because he thought an advisory panel amendment would pass anyway, and he wanted to make sure it would be acceptable to the committee), expressed second thoughts about it. "I want to say one more thing. I think that Congress has loused up this Government beyond redemption because of their appointing committees, committees, committees. We would not be in all this damned trouble if we had not started appointing committees and agencies back in 1934," said Goldwater.

Senator Bumpers defended his amendment, noting that it was a "sense-of-the-Senate" amendment that would not mandate the appointment of the board. But he claimed that more efforts were needed to educate the Senate about decisions costing taxpayers billions of dollars. Wilson's argument prevailed and the Senate rejected the amendment by a margin of 38 to 49.

By voice vote, the Senate adopted a Pressler amendment expressing the sense of the Senate that the president should continue consultations with the governments of the NATO organization concerning the SDI. "The SDI debate is a debate concerning a dramatic change in our whole system of defense and nuclear strategy," Pressler explained. "These changes cannot be made without working closely with our NATO allies."

Amendments by Senators Mathias and Proxmire were also adopted. These amendments required reports on the impact of SDI expenditures on military research and military projects and a study of the impact of SDI expenditures on the civilian economy.

The amendment by Senator Proxmire established two criteria to be met before a space defense system could be deployed: The defense system must be both survivable and cost effective. The criteria were the same as those already set by the administration, and the amendment was agreed to by a voice vote.

At this point, it was nearly 2:00 a.m., and the Senate agreed to recess until later in the day. When the action resumed on June 5, 1985, a motion to reconsider the vote by which the Bumpers SDI advisory panel amendment had been defeated was the pending business.[23]

Senators Goldwater and Nunn announced their willingness to appoint consultants to advise the Armed Services Committee and the Senate as a whole on the SDI. This arrangement was satisfactory to Senators Bumpers and Levin, and the motion to reconsider the advisory panel amendment was tabled. This ended the May–June 1985 round of U.S. Senate debate on the SDI.

Throughout the debate, the Armed Services Committee clearly possessed the votes necessary to defeat any amendment that would cut the recommended level of SDI funding or alter the program in any major way. That President Reagan had seized control of the issue was beyond refute. Still, the Senate debate illustrated many questions that remain unanswered. The Senate's approval of a large increase in SDI funding appeared in large part attributable to the negotiations in Geneva and the belief that some type of arms control agreement was attainable. To the extent that these conditions change, the future of the SDI is still uncertain. The defeat of the Wallop amendment also demonstrated that many senators who approve research may have second thoughts about actual deployment. Such deployments are not contemplated until well into the future, and it is clear that there will be many more congressional debates on the SDI. Nonetheless, the $2.97 billion funding level for fiscal year 1986 and the absence of micromanagement provisions dictated by Congress represented a victory for the Reagan administration and SDI proponents.

Floor action on the SDI in the House of Representatives occurred on June 20, 1985, during consideration of the Department of Defense authorization bill for fiscal year 1986. Earlier, the House Armed Services Committee had held closed hearings over six days on SDI-related issues. The Appropriations Subcommittee on Defense held closed hearings two days in May concerning the SDI and other defense spending issues.

Armed Services Chairman Les Aspin (D-Wisc.) introduced H.R. 1872, the authorization bill approved by his committee, on May 15, 1985. He announced the committee's approval of $2.5 billion for SDI research, $1.2 billion less than that requested by the administration. He reported that the committee had considered and rejected several amendments to either increase or reduce funding for the program.[24] Several of these amendments were offered again, and once again were rejected, on the House floor on June 20.[25]

Ten amendments relating to the SDI were considered by the House, of which three were adopted and one rejected by voice votes. Of the six amendments on which roll call votes occurred, only one survived—and that was an amendment embodying the Armed Services Committee's $2.5 billion funding recommendation. Offering the committee recommendation as a floor amendment might appear to be redundant, but that action helped to focus the debate and alternative amendments on the committee position while giving members of the House a clear sense of the full range of proposed funding levels.

The debate began with three amendments that were disposed of by voice vote. They were offered by Congressmen Charles Bennett (D-Fla.), Kenneth Kramer (R-Colo.), and Duncan Hunter (R-Calif.).

Bennett's amendment, in his words, "requires the Secretary of Defense to report to Congress, at the time of next year's budget request, on the probable Soviet responses to the full deployment of star wars weapons." The amendment specified five areas to be examined by the secretary: (1) the possibility of Soviet action to overwhelm strategic defenses by deploying additional offensive weapons; (2) the potential for evasion of strategic defenses by cruise missiles or low-trajectory submarine-launched missiles; (3) the vulnerability of such a system to ASAT weapons; (4) the wisdom of sharing SDI findings with the Soviets; and (5) the estimated cost of a completed SDI system from research through deployment.

Representative Bennett cited skeptical hearing testimony from General Brent Scowcroft and former Defense Secretaries James Schlesinger and Harold Brown as justification for requiring additional information on the above areas to "help Congress scientifically evaluate the benefits and drawbacks of the strategic defense initiative." With no opposition, the Bennett reporting requirement amendment was adopted.

Representative Kramer's amendment to provide an additional $524.5 million for the SDI by canceling the Midgetman small ICBM program then was rejected quickly by voice vote. Kramer said, "We can make the current generation of strategic offensive nuclear weapons—MX, Trident, D-5, B1-B—the last of its kind. We can take funding now earmarked for the follow-on generation of strategic offensive systems—of which the so-called Midgetman ICBM is the vanguard—and redirect that funding into the Strategic Defense Initiative Research Program."

Speaking for the committee in opposition to the amendment, Representative Dave McCurdy (D-Okla.) reminded the House that "Henry Kissinger was one of the leading proponents of moving away from a MIRV'd capability to a single warhead missile, which is far more stable . . . than having a . . . MIRV'd rocket with a lot of warheads sitting in a vulnerable position. After the action of the House this week to cap the MX funding, . . . I think it is necessary to move forward on the small mobile missile."

Claiming to be a strong supporter of the SDI, Representative Elwood Hillis (R-Ind.) opposed the Kramer amendment on the grounds that the Midgetman system "also was strongly recommended by the President's Commission on Strategic Forces and identified as a key element of future arms control negotiations."

Immediately following rejection of the Kramer amendment, Representative McCurdy proposed an amendment to increase funding of the Midgetman by $150 million. Kramer, the lone opposing speaker, restated his opposition to deployment of a new generation of strategic offensive weapons. He condemned the Midgetman program for violating the SALT II agreement and labeled it an "absolutely impractical" counter to heavy Soviet missiles. Several members refuted these arguments, and the McCurdy amendment was approved by voice vote.

Representative Duncan Hunter's amendment encouraged the president to "seek the cooperation and participation of United States' allies in the research and development of technologies that would assist in the Strategic Defense Initiative," including joint ventures with private firms, but it also required safeguards "to protect critical technologies from unauthorized transfer to nonalliance nations." Despite a reminder from Representative Samuel S. Stratton (D-N.Y.) that recent allied reactions to the SDI had been critical, the Hunter amendment was approved by a voice vote.

At this point, Representative Melvin Price (D-Ill.) offered the committee amendment establishing SDI funding for fiscal year 1986 at $2.5 billion. Without intervening debate, Representative Marjorie Holt (R-Md.) immediately offered her amendment to raise that amount to $2,962,962,000—almost identical to the Senate-approved funding level.

Representative Ron Dellums (D-Calif.) then introduced his amendment to reduce funding to $955 million and to require consistency of SDI activities with the ABM treaty. Dellums expressed strong opposition to the SDI program, arguing that it would be an imperfect defense, would threaten the ABM treaty, would be too expensive, and was based on misguided logic. Specific programs eliminated by his amendment covered activities that he maintained could potentially violate the ABM treaty sometime in the future. The amendment would have allowed only basic research to continue, precluding all tests and demonstrations. Dellums insisted that the SDI would create a situation where a first-strike attack on the United States would be more tempting. This would create, according to Dellums, a high-technology arms race. He argued that "by pushing for the expansion of the arms race into a new technological area, we risk losing what may be one of our final opportunities to negotiate our way out from beneath the threat of nuclear annihilation."

"As Carl Sagan summarized this morning, other than the fact that the SDI system can be underflown, overwhelmed, outfoxed, cannot be run by humans but only by computers, would breach a number of arms control treaties and could trigger a thermal nuclear war, other than that, . . . it is not a bad system," said Dellums.

Following a short colloquy between Congressmen Dellums and John Conyers (D-Mich.), who also spoke in support of the lowest SDI funding proposal of the day, Representative Jim Courter (R-N.J.) offered an amendment to Holt's amendment that would provide full funding of the administration's $3.7 billion request—$800 million above Holt's proposal.

Courter stressed the virtues of abandoning the strategic doctrine of MAD. He questioned the "twisted logic" of a policy that assumed that nuclear weapons would always be controlled by rational decision makers who would never make mistakes, saying, "I am suggesting that the research and development that we are asking for may lead us to a safer world . . . away from the doctrine of mutually assured destruction. And that alternative is doing the robust research that is necessary in the strategic defense initiative to determine whether we can deploy defenses—star shield, not star wars—defend ourselves through nonnuclear, nonthreatening devices that would not be used unless and until a warhead was aimed and coming toward our homeland, would not be activated until that case."

Representative Jack Kemp (R-N.Y.) countered the view that SDI research and development would provoke potential U.S. adversaries. He said, "That is the moral equivalent of telling a policeman or a fireman that if he or she were to put on a bulletproof vest that it would somehow be provocative to the criminal or to the pyromaniac."

Congressman Courter also raised the issue of Soviet strategic defense activities: "According to the best estimates of our Government, they are spending as much on strategic defenses as they are on strategic offensive weapons. . . . They have 10,000 scientists, 2 of which are Nobel laureates, that are involved in only laser technology, for the purposes of using laser technology to defend themselves against intercontinental ballistic missiles." Asserting that the Soviet Union had deployed 10,000 surface-to-air missiles, some of which might have ABM capabilities, he asked, "We, the United States; how many surface-to-air missiles do we have? Zero. The Soviet Union has over 1,200 interceptors; we have 300. The Soviet Union has 8,000 radars for the purposes of defending their homeland; we have 116. The Soviet Union has 100 antiballistic missile launchers around Moscow; more spares. What do we have as far as [an] ABM? We do not have any at all."

The question of Soviet defensive capabilities was also addressed by Representative Samuel Stratton (D-N.Y.), who cited hearing testimony "that the Soviet Union has already spent between $10 and $15 billion on its own SDI program." Representative John Kasich (R-Ohio) added that "the Soviets have deployed satellites with early detection capability; three over-the-horizon radars . . . ll hen house radars, which are large phased-array radars . . . six Krasnoyarsk-type radars; one of them violates the ABM Treaty; they are battle-management capable; they can track missiles, they can send messages to other systems."

Congressmen Dellums and Kemp engaged in a brief dialogue concerning the comparative worth of nuclear defense. Dellums argued, "I think that many of us have great difficulty understanding the basic principle of ABM, that the best nuclear defense is no nuclear defense. The best nuclear defense is constructive negotiations. That is what this whole thing is about." Kemp insisted that the higher moral ground belonged to proponents of a defensive strategy designed to save lives rather than take them. He also maintained that an arms buildup by the Soviet Union had created an unstable environment. Real arms reduction, he asserted, "becomes politically and strategically possible for the first time" once strategic defenses have rendered nuclear weapons obsolete.

Representative Courter concluded his presentation by returning to the monetary issue: "So the point to keep in mind here is that if the President never spoke, if we never had an Office of Strategic Defense, we would be spending in 1986 between $2.5 billion and $2.8 billion. So a $3.7 billion amendment is a 30 percent increase. . . . Anything below 2.8 or 2.5 is a negative response to the President's request."

Representative Patricia Schroeder (D-Colo.), who earlier had labeled star wars as an "illusion," disagreed with Courter on the capacity of the defense research community to spend a major increase in SDI research dollars. She said, "Everybody in the world has said we cannot increase the amount for research much more than 25 percent in any one year and have it absorbed efficiently. . . . A lot of the money we have already put in the pipeline still has not been spent."

Representative Nicholas Mavroules (D-Mass.) spoke on behalf of his amendment to freeze SDI funding at the $1.4 billion level. He maintained that this would "ensure that all research is conducted in a manner consistent with the 1972 Anti-Ballistic Missile Treaty. And it would prohibit fiscal year 1986 spending on demonstration projects or non-laboratory testing." While stating support for "broad and vigorous research as the President stated in March," he warned, "Before we move away from the doctrine of deterrence, we must define what we expect to accomplish with SDI and any weapons in space."

Mavroules added these comments on his amendment's prohibition against demonstration tests: "Many of these demonstrations bump up against the 1972 Anti-Ballistic Missile Treaty. If we are to renounce the ABM agreement, or move toward strategic defense rather than strategic deterrence, that decision must be deliberate and intentional. It should not simply be based on the fact that prototypes are built, tested—and, here's the danger, deployed."

Congressman Hunter's response to that reasoning emphasized a distinction between testing weapons systems and testing weapons concepts: "It is not our job to act as advocates for Soviet lawyers or to take the legal points that they might be expected to take under the ABM Treaty. It is quite clear that the ABM Treaty constrains us from testing the actual systems or prototypes of those systems, or components of those systems. It does not constrain us from testing concepts. If it constrained us from testing concepts, then . . . the homing overlay missile experiment . . . would be violative of ABM, because that test, the concept of whether or not you can in fact defend a country against an incoming missile, is relevant to missile defense. . . .

"If it is illegal for us to bump up against any concepts that have some . . . defense against missiles, then in fact our defense support program violates the ABM Treaty because it is based on our capability to locate and be aware of Soviet missiles when they take off on a course for the United States."

Congressman Kramer returned to the question of costs: "Many have argued that this will not be cheap. The price of peace has never been cheap. . . .

"Some, such as the Fletcher Commission, suggest $100 billion. Some of the detractors, the people opposed to this program, give us numbers like $1 trillion.

"But do you realize that . . . our country alone in the past 25 years has spent at least $1 trillion and possibly $2 trillion on nuclear weapons and weapons of mass destruction? If you compare that cost to the central cost of implementing SDI and recognize also that whether we do SDI or not very well may determine the future of civilization on this planet, I submit that the cost, whether it be $100 billion or $1 trillion, is a cost we simply cannot afford not to pay."

Still, there were members who were troubled by the magnitude of these cost estimates. Representative Pat Williams (D-Mont.) said, "We have some legitimate questions about star wars and perhaps in this time of budget deficits we should ask the important question first. What is it going to cost? . . . The taxpayers of this country need to think about that and so does this Congress, because a trillion dollars is what we now spend for all Federal spending. Are we really going to spend that on just one system?"

Representative Norman Dicks (D-Wash.) explained his amendment in this fashion: "It would lower the committee level of funding from $2.5 billion to $2.1 billion, but most importantly it has some very important limitations on the money that can be spent so that we stay in compliance with the ABM agreement. . . .

"First would be on the airborne optical system. This project would conduct a test in 1988, using funds requested in this bill. This test appears to be inconsistent with provisions of the ABM Treaty prohibiting the development, testing or deployment of airbased ABM components.

"This does not cut out the money; it holds it at last year's level, on each of these items, which is a substantial amount of money. The second project is the space-based hypervelocity launcher. This project would conduct a test in space after 1990, using hypervelocity miniature kill vehicle projectiles for space-based boost phase and midcourse defense. The administration argues that this test will be against an antisatellite device. But it would have the same characteristics as a missile warhead, something the United States has stated in prior years would be a treaty violation.

"The third demonstration restricted at last year's level of funding would be the space-based kinetic kill vehicle. This project would demonstrate after 1990 a space-based rocket-propelled miniature kill vehicle interception system. It faces the same ABM Treaty problems as the hypervelocity launcher.

"And, finally, the space-based laser. One of the major tasks under this project is the acquisition, tracking, and pointing task. It is the successor to Talon Gold which was substantially cut and restructured last year by the administration. Its demonstration would violate the ABM agreement on space-based ABM components.

"The other areas that we would demand that there be full funding of would be system survivability, lethality and target hardening, battle management, command, control and communications, and SDI systems architecture. Plus under my amendment we would add $75 million to look at the very important question of if we go ahead with SDI—and I think we should not prejudge that at this point—what do we do against bombers and cruise missiles, a very important threat? This amendment would add $75 million."

Representative Larry Combest (R-Tex.), however, argued: "When you cut the request, when you limit what we can find out, you equally limit our options for the future. The difference in $2 billion and $3.7 billion in research may well mean the difference in success and failure. . . . The committee level of funding for SDI would be more defensible if it were a pool of money which could be applied to the various areas of research as warranted by the research itself. But cutting back funding in specific areas while not knowing exactly what the needs will be just doesn't make sense."

As the House concluded its six-hour debate on SDI funding, it was apparent that the members were concerned with five general issues: the feasibility of a missile defense system, the cost of such a system, the capacity of the Pentagon to effectively spend a major funding increase on research, potential Soviet responses, and the impact of the program on the ABM treaty and arms control negotiations. For some, there were clear enough answers to the questions raised in the debate to justify their votes. Other members of the House were less certain of the answers to the questions that the SDI research program was designed to probe. In any event, a clear majority favored continuation of the research effort, knowing that a future Congress would be faced with more difficult judgments on the ultimate questions of testing and deployment.

Following defeat of the Dellums amendment by a vote of 102 to 320, the House successively defeated the Mavroules amendment by 155 to 268, the Courter amendment by 104 to 315, the Dicks amendment by 195 to 221, and the Holt amendment by 169 to 242. The Price amendment, reaffirming the Armed Services Committee recommendation of $2.5 billion, was then adopted by a vote of 256 to 150.

On June 26, 1985, the House resumed consideration of the fiscal year 1986 defense authorization bill and dispensed with several additional amendments relating to the SDI and ASAT weapons.[26]

Representative George Brown (D-Calif.), who had authored the House-passed ASAT testing moratorium amendment in 1984, offered an amendment to prohibit testing of a U.S. ASAT weapon against an object in space until the president certified the Soviets had conducted such a test on a dedicated ASAT weapon after the date of enactment of the Defense Authorization Act. Legislation enacted in 1984 had permitted three tests in fiscal year 1985 against points, but not objects, in space. It would permit tests against objects in space, too, under requirements described earlier in this chapter. Two successful tests were conducted in 1984, with ten more planned by the Defense Department.

The House Armed Services Committee had approved funding of the ASAT program with no limitations on testing. Congressman Brown asserted his support for a vigorous ASAT research program, commenting that "the first likely technological product of SDI will be an effective antisatellite weapon, since satellites in low Earth orbit are easier to kill than missiles."[27] However, he argued that the United States would be more secure if weapons were not deployed in space. He also expressed concern that the technology employed in the U.S. F-15-launched ASAT might be obsolete. On the latter point, he referred to a Defense Department report[28] that stressed the Soviets' progress in developing prototype ground-based laser weapons that could be targeted on U.S. satellites. Brown recommended switching the $4.5 billion needed for initial deployment of the F-15-launched ASAT to laser research.

Other arguments advanced on behalf of the Brown ASAT testing limitation amendment included the following:

1. The Soviet ASAT is unreliable and is not a serious threat to critical U.S. satellites.
2. Advances in satellite-protective techniques make even low-orbit satellites defensible against Soviet or U.S. ASATs.
3. An ASAT testing limitation would enhance opportunities for the negotiation of an ASAT arms control agreement.

Principal arguments against the Brown amendment included the following:

1. Only the Soviets possess an operational, reliable ASAT.
2. The existing Soviet system and ground-based ASAT laser weapons potentially threaten U.S. reconnaissance capability.
3. Continuation of ASAT testing under existing requirements or conditions provides the best leverage to obtain an ASAT arms control agreement.

4. Excessive constraints on ASAT systems interfere with BMD research under the SDI.

Representative Steny Hoyer (D-Md.) offered an amendment to the Brown amendment that authorized an additional $20 million for the Air Force Space System Survivability Program, which includes research on satellite-protective technology. Both critics and supporters of the underlying Brown testing limitation amendment endorsed Hoyer's amendment, which was accepted by a voice vote. The Brown amendment then passed by 229 to 193.

By voice vote, the House also approved an amendment by Representative Thomas Foglietta (D-Pa.), modified by an amendment by Representative Robert Badham (R-Calif.), prohibiting SDI funds from being used for advanced development, demonstration, testing, or evaluation of the use of weapons powered by nuclear explosions in space in a manner inconsistent with specified space arms control agreements.

Representative Aspin then offered as one amendment a series of amendments that included two requested by Congressmen Foglietta and Hunter establishing SDI study commissions.[29] One established the Congressional Commission on Strategic Defense, composed of eight members of Congress selected by the bipartisan leadership of both houses and charged with a comprehensive analysis of the SDI and reports to Congress on its findings. The other amendment established the Strategic Defense Initiative Commission to be appointed by the president for the purpose of compiling a report to Congress detailing specific recommendations on key aspects of the SDI. The amendment including creation of these two commissions was approved by a voice vote.

On November 8, 1985, President Reagan signed the act containing a House-Senate compromise authorization of $2.75 billion for the SDI in fiscal year 1986. In December 1985, Congress approved a $2.75 billion appropriation for the SDI for fiscal year 1986. This amount was a compromise between the Senate's appropriation level of $2.96 billion and the House level of $2.5 billion.

8

Treaty Limitations on
Military Space Operations

President Reagan opened a new and complex debate on the intent and effectiveness of the 1972 ABM treaty when he challenged the nation's scientists to devise a ballistic missile system using exotic new technologies. The challenge immediately raised a red flag—did the treaty permit such a system? Critics and supporters of the SDI differ sharply as to where the fine line should be drawn between research and development, on the one hand, and between development and deployment, on the other. Controversy also swirls around the legality under the treaty of ASATs, laser weapons, particle beams, and other new technologies insofar as they have distinct capabilities as ABM (or BMD) systems or components of such systems.

This chapter first summarizes the ABM treaty and looks briefly at other space-related treaties. It then examines the issues at stake by citing authorities on the relationship between the SDI and the ABM treaty.

The ABM treaty constitutes one result of SALT I. The other consists of an interim agreement limiting offensive strategic arms. The purpose of the ABM treaty was to restrict the development and deployment of systems defending against offensive strategic arms. The preamble states that limiting ABM systems "would be a substantial factor in curbing the race in strategic offensive arms and would lead to a decrease in the risk of outbreak of war involving nuclear weapons."

The treaty, although of unlimited duration, is formally reviewed every five years and may be amended. Either party may withdraw from the agreement with six months' prior notice if it decides that "extraordinary events related to the subject matter of the Treaty have jeopardized its supreme interests." The two super-powers reviewed the treaty in 1977 and 1982 without amending it. The treaty does allow each nation one fixed, land-based ABM system as well as the right to carry out modernization and replacement of such ABM system.

Although many observers consider the ABM treaty to be the outstanding arms control achievement to date, there are other treaties that impose limitations on the military uses of space. These include the 1963 Limited Test Ban Treaty, the 1967 Outer Space Treaty, and the 1979 Moon Treaty.[1]

The Limited Test Ban Treaty prohibits nuclear weapons explosions in space or in any other environment if an explosion would produce radioactive debris outside the borders of the country conducting such a test. The Outer Space Treaty prohibits the introduction of nuclear or other weapons of mass destruction into space. It also preserves the use of the moon and other celestial bodies for peaceful purposes. The United States has never signed the 1979 Moon Treaty, which includes a prohibition on military activities, such as the testing and deployment of weapons, on the moon or other celestial bodies. U.S. objections to the Moon Treaty were based on claims that the Outer Space Treaty already guaranteed peaceful uses of space and the celestial bodies. Perhaps more important was the desire to avoid the Moon Treaty's constraints on peaceful exploration and exploitation of space resources. The Soviet Union in 1981 and 1983 offered draft treaties at the United Nations banning all weapons from space, the use of force in space, and all military activities by manned spacecraft and requiring the dismantling of existing ASATs.

It is the ABM treaty, however, that is at the very heart of the SDI controversy since it deals specifically with BMDs. Opponents of the SDI have told various congressional committees that the compelling case for preserving the ABM treaty rests upon the recognition that defensive systems could upset the nuclear stalemate resulting from the strategy of MAD. They argue that the original ABM debate produced the consensus that an ABM system would cost vast sums of money, would soon become obsolete in the face of more effective offensive weapons, and would only increase the arms race. Therefore, arms control on offensive weapons would be the safer, less expensive, and more effective route to security. Supporters of the SDI believe the ABM debate should be reopened because of evolving technologies that are far more advanced than anything previously contemplated. They argue that the Soviets have been vigorously pursuing research in such technologies.

Article V of the treaty prohibits the development, testing, or deployment of sea-based, air-based, space-based, or mobile ABM systems. Ambassador Gerard Smith, the principal U.S. negotiator of the ABM treaty, told the Senate Armed Services Committee on June 28, 1972, that laboratory testing and development were permitted because there was no dependable way to verify such research.[2] In the context of the treaty, he added, development of an ABM system would start "where field testing is initiated on either a prototype or breadboard model."

"It was understood by both sides that the prohibition on development applied to activities involved after a component moves from the laboratory development and testing stage to the field testing stage, wherever performed," Smith said.

He also told the committee that further ABM systems "based on other physical principles" would not be permitted unless the treaty were amended. The term "other physical principles" has been construed as covering laser technologies, he said. Research in laser and other directed-energy technologies is permitted, Smith testified, but field testing and deployment are not, if these are to be space based.

Dr. James C. Fletcher, who headed the president's strategic defense technology panel, addressed these points at a Senate Armed Services Committee hearing on March 8, 1984.[3] Fletcher testified, in part: "Many of my colleagues ask me why we are reopening an issue which they believed was forever closed during the ABM debate. . . . First, I don't believe that the issue was ever closed for the Soviets. The data which we saw . . . provided . . . striking evidence that the Soviet Union has pursued with vigor all of the technologies we have recommended and many which we do not even understand yet. Secondly, those technologies which are essential to a truly effective defense against ballistic missiles are just emerging. In the 1960s and early 1970s we had no way to effectively perform boost-phase intercept; we had insufficient means to discriminate between decoys and warheads; we could not simultaneously manage thousands of engagements; and we were forced to consider the use of nuclear warheads at such low altitudes within the atmosphere that collateral damage to the defended area would have been substantial. Now directed energy and even 'hypervelocity' kinetic energy weapons appear promising for boost-phase intercept. Precision sensors make unambiguous detection and discrimination of warheads from decoys and debris possible. New electronic advances make it possible both to manage tens of thousands of engagements simultaneously, but also, when coupled with precision sensors make it feasible to perform 'hit-to-kill' intercepts without requiring nuclear warheads for the defense. These reasons provided the team with compelling rationales for reexamining the technical issues associated with . . . ballistic missile defense."

Senator Charles H. Percy of Illinois, chairman of the Senate Foreign Relations Committee, earlier spoke for many opponents of the SDI when he made these observations at a committee hearing on April 14, 1983: " As one Senator who vigorously opposed the ABM deployment—and deployment is an entirely different thing—in the late 1960s, I must say that I approach the question of actual deployments of new ABM weapons with considerable skepticism and reserve. . . . We struggled with this problem, the ABM, in the late 1960s. We were searching for the truth, and we reached deep into the scientific community to get all the guidance and help that we possibly could.

"A majority of the Senate and a majority of this committee came to the conclusion . . . that the ABM was not the right system to deploy. If we could mutually agree to not deploy, and it had to be a mutual agreement on both sides and be fully verifiable, we would be better off.

"I don't know what the estimates are, but we would have spent about $150 billion on that system to date. We would have spent billions each and every year to just maintain it and keep it up to date. But it would still have become obsolete.

"I don't know of any decision that we have made that has been proven more accurate and right. I will couple that with saying we have to keep up our research and development constantly in this area."[4]

Ambassador Gerard Smith, another leading critic of the SDI, told the Senate Foreign Relations Committee on June 22, 1983, "Any major program to implement the President's 'dream' would very quickly run afoul of the ABM Treaty's constraints."[5]

"Even engineering work to develop a space-based system is banned," he said. He also testified: "By foreshadowing a program which would inevitably violate the ABM Treaty, I believe that we are introducing uncertainty which cannot fail to have a prejudicial impact on the current strategic balance. . . .

"One prejudicial effect may already be in train. It seems likely that U.S. refusal to negotiate controls over antisatellite systems is motivated by an aim to avoid further restraints on exotic 'star wars' components of defensive systems which would use similar technology. Not only would going for 'star wars' systems signal our intent to annul the ABM Treaty, which for 11 years has staved off a superpower competition in defensive systems to match the present only informally and incompletely regulated race in offensive systems, it would signal to the Soviets a likely aim to neutralize their retaliatory capability to respond to any American first strike. The President himself recognized this danger by saying that, paired with offensive missiles, an effective defense could be viewed as fostering an aggressive policy, and he added that we do not want to give that signal."

At a House Foreign Affairs Committee hearing on May 2, 1984, Smith inveighed against amendments to the ABM treaty. "We hear from the administration talk of possibly amending the ABM Treaty to accommodate the SDI programs," he said. "Since the expressed purpose of the treaty was to ban the very systems that SDI contemplates, the amendment route seems widely impractical as a way to legalize SDI's future. If I would give an analogy, it would be like talking of amending the Volstead Act to permit the sale of liquor."[6]

Defense Secretary Caspar Weinberger, a staunch supporter of the SDI, gave an entirely different assessment of the situation during the NBC television show "The Real Star Wars," which the network aired originally on September 8, 1984. Weinberger asked pointedly, "Do we want to let a treaty which the Soviets are not observing and have violated stand in the way . . . of our ability to develop a thoroughly reliable system of defense which can render their nuclear missiles impotent?"

Weinberger added that the ABM treaty was based on two assumptions, neither of which has proved accurate. "It was based on the assumption that neither side would do anything more with respect to strategic defense. And the Soviets, since 1967, since before the treaty and after the treaty, have continued to work very assiduously and effectively in this field," he said. "The second assumption was that both sides would remain relatively equal in offensive systems, and that hasn't come true either. The Soviets have put in enormous sums and enormous developments, and they're in the fifth generation of deploying their missiles, and we're still on the verge—still debating whether we should have an MX or not. So, neither of the assumptions which undergirded the ABM Treaty have been adhered to."

During congressional debate over the treaty's technicalities, members agonized over the implications of a specific comma in Article I. The article bans "antiballistic missile weapons, currently consisting of launchers, missiles, and radars." Some argued that the comma before "currently" meant that all ABM weapons were banned, and not merely those listed as currently existing. Others disagreed, arguing that such a restriction would render the rest of the treaty useless. Senator Malcolm Wallop of Wyoming, one of the earliest congressional advocates of a BMD, spoke at length about the matter of punctuation and other aspects of the ABM treaty during a Senate Armed Services Committee hearing on May 2, 1983.[7] The Wyoming Republican said, "Some have suggested that the ABM Treaty of 1982 prohibits us from putting laser weapons into space. I have read that treaty, and defy anyone to show me where it says any such thing. In fact, the treaty never mentions directed energy weapons at all, much less does the treaty define them in such a way as to make possible their limitations.

"The first rule of international law is that whatever is not covered explicitly in a treaty is not covered at all. Some argue that because Article I bans antiballistic missile weapons, currently consisting of launchers, missiles, and radars, and that because there is a comma before the word 'currently', everything which could possibly serve to shoot down a missile on a warhead is banned forever. That cannot be so. If it were so, the rest of the treaty would be superfluous.

"The absolutist interpretation of the treaty is also undercut by the Soviet Union's own proposal to the United States in August 1981 for a treaty to ban from space weapons not of mass destruction. Both Leonid Brezhnev and Tass said that such a treaty is necessary because no treaty 'currently in force' bans such weapons.

"I might add that Mr. Andropov reaffirmed that in his response to some of your future witnesses in here, as reported in the Aerospace Daily of May 2, he said no such treaty restrictions presently exist. I would suggest, Mr. Chairman, if they do not think so, we had better not.

"Suppose for a moment that the Soviet Union put a laser weapon in orbit. Would that be a violation of the ABM Treaty? Immediately our Arms Control and Disarmament Agency would ask the Soviets whether the weapon were an ABM weapon. The Soviets would say no, it is an ASAT.

"Then we would see the weapon tested against a missile. But the Soviets could continue to say it is primarily an ASAT. In this instance, there would be no more proof that a violation of the treaty had occurred than there has been in innumerable other cases involving both SALT I and SALT II.

"Are dual purpose air-defense systems violations of SALT I? How can one prove that these systems are not intended primarily for air defense? One can't. Does encryption of missile telemetry violate SALT II? How can one prove with the words of the treaty itself that the encryption impeded verification? I merely note that even these simple cases have proved too complex for us so far.

"In sum, these treaties say what they say. They mean no more than they say.

"An American laser weapon in orbit would certainly violate one view of the ABM Treaty, the view held by those Americans who want this country to accept mutual assured destruction. But an American laser weapon would not be prohibited by the words of the treaty, by the Soviets' understanding of the treaty, or by the standards of compliance with arms control agreements which have evolved over the years."

Dr. Albert Carnesale of Harvard University, who helped negotiate the ABM treaty, gave his overview of the SDI's impact on the 1972 accord during a Senate Foreign Relations Committee hearing on April 25, 1984. Dr. Carnesale was asked if we were on the verge of violating the ABM treaty. He replied, "No; in the short term we are not. There is nothing that I know of in the Strategic Defense Initiative, particularly the new programs, that would violate the treaty in the near term.

"But, certainly, to achieve the ultimate objective of the initiative would require violation of the treaty eventually.

"Let me illustrate the point. There are no limits in the treaty on laboratory research. There are no constraints on research on particle beams or lasers. Indeed, at permitted ABM test sites—of which they are two—you could test fixed, ground-based lasers or particle beams as ABM systems. But to go the next step and put one of these devices in space would be a violation of the treaty. One cannot develop space-based systems or components. And the word 'develop' in the context of the treaty means to build a prototype.

"To proceed all the way down this path would require modification or abrogation of the treaty. But there is no problem in the near term. Indeed, there were programs planned before the Strategic Defense Initiative that probably would have run up against the treaty sooner than the new programs. For example, one of the midcourse intercept schemes used multiple, independently guided interceptor missiles that would home in on different reentry vehicles. Such systems are prohibited by the treaty."[8]

The most sophisticated BMD proposal to precede President Reagan's SDI was the High Frontier project, advanced by Lt. General Daniel Graham (Ret.), former head of the Defense Intelligence Agency. This called for a space-based BMD system using conventional, "off-the-shelf" technology consisting of 432 satellites armed with 40 to 50 miniature homing devices similar to those developed for the U.S. ASAT. The Department of Defense has not endorsed this proposal.

At a Senate Foreign Relations Committee hearing on April 14, 1983, General Graham was asked whether his High Frontier program would have necessitated the abrogation of the ABM treaty.[9] He replied, in effect, that the system could be deployed, but only after discussions with the other side "to see how it will be handled in the treaty." "So, my view: yes, you can deploy this, but you are obliged to sit down and talk about it with the Soviets," he said.

Jan Lodal, former National Security Council staff member, took issue with Graham's view: "This is a very common and very wrong reading of the ABM Treaty, not only its negotiating history but what it says. In fact, it says that 'an ABM system is any system that is designed to counter ballistic missiles in their flight trajectory, currently consisting of—'. And it was written that way on purpose, saying that the general prohibition is what applies in the treaty. The 'currently consisting of' is strictly a description of today's situation.

"What the paragraph says about systems based on new technology . . . it is talking strictly about land-based systems. It doesn't at all interfere with the previous prohibition on space-based systems, which is absolute and comprehensive. It talks about land-based systems that might be based on new technologies, and therefore might not be countable in the same sense as interceptor systems, and says in that case they have to be subject to discussion.

"But that is a further limitation. It is not a broadening of the treaty. And the prohibition on space is absolute."

General Graham provided a conclusion when he said, "Let me cut through that knot. If you want to look at the treaty as a guardhouse lawyer to protect the Soviets against our deploying a space-borne system, you can make the case. If you want to look at the treaty as a guardhouse lawyer figuring out a way to deploy it and not violate the treaty, you can do that, too."[10]

In a report on outer space arms control negotiations, issued in November 1983, the Senate Foreign Relations Committee affirmed its support of the ABM treaty and suggested that BMD research efforts in the United States were sufficient to meet the Soviet threat without the SDI. The report said, in part, "The Committee believes that U.S. interests have been well served by the ABM Treaty. It has saved many billions in acquisition and operations and maintenance costs. Had systems been deployed in the early 1970s, they would be outdated today and additional expenditures would have been required to modernize or replace them. The treaty has helped to avert a defense planner's nightmare by avoiding contests in defensive systems and in offensive technologies designed to defeat them. Conditions created by the Treaty provide incentives for implementing current strategic arms control proposals in which MIRVed missiles would be abandoned in favor of more stable single warhead systems.

"Since research activities are not fully verifiable under the terms of the accord, the Committee believes that vigilance through an active ABM research program is a necessary guarantee against Soviet breakthrough. Absent evidence to the contrary, proposals reportedly under consideration by the Administration appear to go well beyond the level of effort required in guarding against this contingency. These proposals call for a level of effort that would permit a U.S. deployment decision rather than simply a hedge against a Soviet deployment."[11]

The president's Commission on Strategic Forces, also known as the Scowcroft Commission after its chairman, General Brent Scowcroft, drew a similar conclusion about the SDI vis-à-vis the ABM treaty. In a letter to the president dated March 21, 1984, the commission said, "Ballistic missile defense is a critical aspect of the strategic balance and therefore is central to arms control. One of the most successful arms control agreements is the Anti-Ballistic Missile Treaty of 1972. That fact should not be allowed to obscure the possibility that technological developments at some point could make it in the interests of both sides to amend the current treaty. . . . However, no move in the direction of the deployment of active defense should be made without the most careful consideration of the possible strategic and arms control implications.

". . . In the Commission's view, research permitted by the ABM Treaty is important in order to ascertain the realistic possibilities which technology might offer, as well as to guard against the possibility of an ABM breakout by the other side. But the strategic implications of ballistic missile defense and the criticality of the ABM Treaty to further arms control agreements dictate extreme caution in proceeding to engineering development in this sensitive area."[12]

Perhaps the clearest explanation to emerge from the various interpretations of the ABM treaty was offered at the OTA Space Arms Control Workshop, held in Washington in January 1984. The following is excerpted from the workshop proceedings, published in May 1984: "An antiballistic missile system is defined, for the purposes of the treaty, as 'a system to counter strategic ballistic missiles or their elements in flight trajectory'. This phrase is followed by the words 'currently consisting of' and then a list of three items: ABM interceptor missiles, ABM launchers, and ABM radars. The treaty is not restricted to those systems. It says what the current systems are, but it is intended to cover all ABM systems.

"Note that the definition refers to strategic weapons. Systems to counter tactical missiles are not covered at all—'a loophole that we designed carefully, and which they are pushing through', according to a panelist. Note also that the treaty defines an ABM as a system to counter strategic weapons. It does not say 'system designed to counter', as the Soviets would have liked, nor does it read 'system capable of countering', which was the United States' preferred wording. The United States was concerned that, by upgrading surface-to-air missiles (SAMs), the U.S.S.R. would be able to deploy a considerable ABM capability. The Soviet Union, on the other hand, was concerned that it would be forced to classify some 10,000 SAMs as ABM interceptors. The analogy of upgrading ASAT weapons to give them ABM capability is similarly covered by the treaty.

"This definition is essentially a capability test. All systems which are ABM-capable, whether or not they were designed for that purpose, are either considered ABM systems under the treaty or else are in violation of Article VI(a), which prohibits giving ABM capability to non-ABM systems. This article was 'really aimed at SAM systems', explained a panelist, 'but the same thing applies to ASAT systems'. If an ASAT weapon is given the ability to counter strategic ballistic missiles, then 'it's a violation or else it's got to count as an ABM system, one way or the other'. . . .

"The ABM treaty prohibits all ABM deployments which are not explicitly permitted. Article III bans all deployments other than two sites (amended by a 1974 protocol to one) on each side, each having restricted numbers of interceptors, launchers, and radars. These prohibitions, interpreted a panelist, are clear: 'Can you deploy lasers? No. Can you deploy particle beams? No. Can you deploy squizzle dumps or freeble dobbles? No'.

"Article IV permits testing, at designated test sites, of certain systems not deployable under Article III. However, systems permitted at test sites or deployments are severely constrained by Article V, in which 'each party undertakes not to develop, test, or deploy ABM systems or components which are sea-based, air-based, space-based, or mobile land-based'. Only fixed, land-based systems can be tested, and only specified fixed, land-based systems can be deployed. 'Development', as referred to in this provision, was defined in a statement to Congress by the chief U.S. negotiator of the ABM treaty: 'It is understood by both sides that the prohibition on development applies to activities involved after a component moves from the laboratory development testing stage to the field testing stage, wherever performed'. Interpreted by a workshop panelist, 'if

I see one outside the laboratory—a prototype, a bread-board model—if I see one, it's a violation. I don't have to see it tested'. The second part of Article V prohibits a launcher from being able to fire more than one interceptor or be reloaded rapidly.

"Upgrades are prohibited in Article VI(a), as discussed above. No non-ABM systems shall be given ABM capability or be tested in an ABM mode. The second part (b) of Article VI restricts ABM battle management radars by requiring early warning radars to be on the periphery of the country and oriented outwards. Agreed Statement F, approved by U.S. and U.S.S.R. delegation heads at the same time that the treaty was signed, excludes radars used 'for the purposes of tracking objects in outer space or for use as national technical means of verification' from the location and orientation restrictions in Article VI(b).

"Article XII prohibits interference with verification of the treaty, both by banning interference with the national technical means used for verification and by prohibiting 'deliberate concealment measures' which would impede verification by national technical means. Article XIII establishes the Standing Consultative Commission to handle questions relating to treaty compliance, to consider possible amendments, and to consider proposals for further limiting strategic arms.

"Agreed Statement D of the ABM treaty discusses components based on 'other physical principles' and capable of substituting for interceptors, launchers, or radars. Capability, again, is crucial. If a new device can substitute for a launcher, interceptor, or radar, its deployment is prohibited. If it is instead only an adjunct or supplement, it would be permitted. This article specifies that 'specific limitations' on such new systems and their components would be 'subject to discussion' in the Standing Consultative Commission, and that such discussion might lead to amendment of the treaty. Only if the treaty were amended to permit these new components would their deployment be allowed; otherwise, they are prohibited."[13]

These interpretations of ABM treaty limitations on the SDI led Congress in 1984 to require a report from the Department of Defense detailing that department's responses to the treaty issue as well as other congressional concerns.

Appendix B of the report, which was submitted to Congress in classified and unclassified versions in April 1985, is entitled "The Strategic Defense Initiative (SDI) and the ABM Treaty." It addresses the compliance question in the following manner: "There are three major points to be made regarding United States Policy on compliance with the ABM Treaty.

"First, the SDI research program is being conducted in a manner fully consistent with all U.S. Treaty obligations. The President has directed that the program be formulated in a fully compliant manner and the DoD [Department of Defense] has planned and reviewed the program (and will continue to do so) to ensure that it remains compliant. Specifically, our review has found that the research necessary to support a decision on the potential utility of the SDI technology can be conducted in accordance with U.S. Treaty obligations.

"Second, because there are gray areas that are not fully defined in the ABM Treaty, it is necessary in some cases to set additional standards to make certain that the U.S. is in compliance.* This review has been conducted using reasonable standards of U.S. compliance. Four of the more important working principles of this review are that:

- Compliance must be based on objective assessments of capabilities which support a single standard for both sides and not on subjective judgments as to intent which could lead to a double standard of compliance.
- The ABM Treaty prohibits the development, testing, and deployment of ABM systems and components that are space-based, air-based, sea-based, or mobile land-based. However, that agreement does permit research short of field testing of a prototype ABM system or component. This is the type of research that will be conducted under the SDI program.
- New technologies and devices should not be subjected to stricter standards than have evolved for existing systems.
- The ABM Treaty, of course, restricts defenses against strategic ballistic missiles; it does not apply to defenses against nonstrategic ballistic missiles or cruise missiles.

"Third, this report does not consider Soviet violations of the ABM Treaty. We do reserve the right to respond to those violations in appropriate ways, some of which may eventually bear on the Treaty constraints as they apply to the United States. The United States Government must guard against permitting a double standard of compliance, under which the Soviet Government would expect to get away with various violations of arms agreements while the U.S. continues to abide with all provisions."[14]

---

*"An example is the issue of components versus subcomponents. ABM components are defined in the Treaty as currently consisting of ABM missiles, launchers, and radars. Subcomponents, which are not limited by the Treaty, are not defined by the Treaty."

The report added, "The SDI research program can be conducted in a fully compliant manner to reach a decision point in the early 1990s on whether to proceed to development and deployment of an SDI-related system. . . . Development and deployment, given a decision to proceed, would almost certainly require modifications to the ABM Treaty."[15]

The report also indicated the Department of Defense had issued compliance directives and guidelines to ensure continuing compliance with U.S. international agreements. The guidelines require the SDI Office "to submit quarterly reports certifying its compliance and to monitor its projects, as required of other DoD Agencies. The Services are to ensure the SDI projects under their auspices are monitored and implemented in a Treaty compatible manner."

The three categories of scheduled treaty-compliant activities identified in the report were (1) conceptual design or laboratory testing, (2) "field testing" of devices that are not ABM components or prototypes of ABM components, and (3) "field testing" of fixed, land-based ABM components.

9

Strategic Implications

The introduction of the SDI almost immediately brought about a debate inside Congress and among the general public. At issue was the heart of national security—U.S. strategic doctrine. Should the nation continue in the present situation of MAD, or proceed to develop the foundations for a new situation as the president had advocated—mutually assured security (MAS)? MAD relies upon a balance of offensive nuclear weapons between the United States and the Soviet Union to maintain peace. The new concept promised a BMD that would render many, most, or all missile-delivered nuclear weapons obsolete.

This chapter examines some of the key aspects of the projected changes that the SDI might make in U.S. defense strategy. It includes discussion of the overall theory behind MAD, the need for continued ICBM forces even with the SDI, the Hoffman Report's defense of the strategy behind the SDI and comments upon its arms control impact, the effect of the SDI on terrorists' use of nuclear weapons, the degree of protection offered by the SDI, the possibility of a Soviet preemptive strike against a U.S. BMD system, and the risks of relying on computers.

Senator Malcolm Wallop (R-Wyo.) delivered the following stinging attack on the MAD situation in May 1983 before the Senate Armed Services Committee: "Since the days of Robert McNamara, the Pentagon has led the U.S. Government in the strategic policy of mutual assured destruction. This policy has proved to be politically disastrous. The American people have been told that, for the sake of peace, we must forever remain without any protection whatever against Soviet ballistic missiles and that if, for whatever reason, a major war is ever imposed upon us, all of us are sure to die.

"Reasonable people have asked the consequent question: Why do we have to pay billions for our own Armed Forces if these forces will not be able to protect our lives?

"The answer: The function of our strategic forces is to inflict terrible casualties on Russian society.

"As anyone but Mr. McNamara's supporters could have predicted, the American people, who greatly respected their men in uniform when these were protectors, became less and less enthusiastic about them in their brave new roles of 'avengers'.

"Look at contemporary antimilitary movements. At their core, you will find this assertion: Our military forces will not contribute to our safety. And buildup on our part can only raise the already super-abundant likelihood of death and destruction for all.

"Behind today's antimilitary movements lies the kernel of truth that contemporary strategic policy is both militarily senseless and immoral. Not surprisingly, that plea has not been well accepted, support for our own military activities has continued to decline, and the modernization of our strategic forces has lagged shamefully.

"The military consequences of our adherence to MAD have been even worse than political ones. As everyone should know, the Soviets never accepted MAD. Their strategic forces have been built from the ground up, to attack our strategic forces—not to destroy us, but to disarm us."[1]

Wallop then offered the committee his analysis of the Soviet defense arsenal and advised that "the Soviets are spending anywhere from 3 to 5 times as much as we are to develop directed energy weapons."

Senator Wallop provided this solution to the problems presented by the Soviet defense buildup: "Unless we try to outbuild the Soviets in counterforce warheads—which no one proposes and I doubt we could do—we are left with but one possibility: To degrade the usefulness of the Soviet Union's superior missiles by ballistic missile defense. . . .

"The Congress has a responsibility to decide this basic question: Should the American people have the best protection against Soviet ballistic missiles which our ingenuity can devise, or shall we instead, again commit ourselves to remain undefended and rely for our safety on threats of vengeance? . . .

"If we decide it is good to protect ourselves, then it makes sense to build a variety of protective weapons as quickly as possible. If the first editions are not perfect, surely the subsequent ones will be better.

"If, on the other hand, we decide it is not good to protect ourselves, then even near-perfect protective weapons would be a total waste of effort. The political question is logically prior to the technical ones. Our approach to technical matters depends on how the political question is decided."

Following his brief review of promising developments in chemical laser research, Wallop concluded, "In short, there is every reason to believe that we could put a 10-megawatt, 10-meter chemical laser in orbit well before the end of this decade."

Senator William Armstrong's (R-Colo.) following statement echoed Wallop's theme that the issue facing Congress was one of political commitment to the goal of abolishing the immoral situation of MAD. His testimony summarized the failure of previous political regimes that did not modernize their defense establishments to meet the challenges of technologically more advanced opponents: "In reading military history, I am impressed that over and over again, nations have come to historical intersections; those nations which have chosen wisely have survived and prospered while those which have taken wrong turns have paid a bitter price for their errors of judgment.

"The failure of King Philip II to adapt to Mediterranean style naval warfare doomed Spanish efforts to compete in the Atlantic against the English and Dutch and contributed heavily to the historic defeat of the Spanish Armada.

"The conscious and obstinate refusal of the Turks to adopt European methods of training led to one military disaster after another. Even subsequent efforts to modernize could not prevent defeats which culminated in dissolution of the Empire in 1918.

"Similarly, the deliberate downplaying of artillery doomed the ambitions of Frederick the Great despite the legendary valor and obedience of his Prussian troops.

"But the willingness to form a national bank to finance naval expansion permitted Britain to become a global seapower, far outdistancing rival nations including some whose warships were better designed than their British equivalents and whose governments aspired to naval parity or predominance.

"In our own century, drastic strategic mistakes have repeatedly been the margin between safety and suffering, victory and defeat as the French sought to hide behind an impractical Maginot line, the British failed to mobilize against Hitler and America dallied while Japan prepared war in the Pacific.

"That such decisions—of preparedness and strategy—are matters of life or death is the repetitious lesson of history. Therefore President Reagan's March 23rd message to the American people should be evaluated in such an historical perspective.

"Mr. Reagan's proposal is to execute a 180 degree shift in the strategic nuclear policy which the United States has followed for the past twenty years—to move away from a policy based on our ability to kill the Russian people, and toward a policy based on our ability to protect our own homeland without threatening the Russian population. He seeks nothing less than to lift from above our heads the nuclear sword of Damocles. If he is successful in this noble endeavor, I believe President Reagan will one day be regarded as the greatest peacemaker of our century. He deserves our wholehearted admiration and our vigorous support.

"Undoubtedly the Committee will be hearing much testimony of a scientific nature and properly so. But the basic issue of U.S. strategy hinges on issues of moral and political judgment which far transcend purely military or scientific considerations."[2]

Senator Armstrong's closing remarks constituted a powerful condemnation of MAD: "By adhering to the MAD doctrine, we have assured our own destruction in the event of a general nuclear war, but not that of the Soviet Union. The Soviets are on the verge of achieving, if they haven't already, the ability, under conditions of first strike, to destroy virtually all of our ICBMs, virtually all of our strategic bombers, and those nuclear submarines that are in port at any given time. While still most unlikely, a nuclear Pearl Harbor is now a conceivable policy option for the generals in the Kremlin.

"Another fundamental flaw of Mutual Assured Destruction is that it was never mutual. Soviet leaders, in both official statements for foreign consumption and in their military journals, derided it from the beginning as both insane and immoral. As you know, Mr. Chairman, for the MAD doctrine to have any validity at all, it is necessary for the leaders of both the United States and the Soviet Union to reject nuclear war as an instrument of policy. We, of course, have done so. But the Soviet leaders never have. On the contrary, it is still Soviet doctrine that a military clash between the Communist world and the capitalist world is inevitable, that 'weapons of mass destruction' will be used in that clash, and that the Soviets should initiate the use of 'weapons of mass destruction' in order to make certain that the Socialist World will emerge triumphant.

"I don't believe this is more rhetoric on the part of the Soviet leaders, Mr. Chairman. They've been putting their money where their mouths are. The Soviet strategic forces, unlike ours, are configured for an attack on our weapons, not for the mutual massacre of civilians called for in the MAD doctrine. While Secretary McNamara and his successors deliberately stripped America's air defenses so our civilians would be more vulnerable to Soviet nuclear weapons, the Soviets were spending hundreds of billions of rubles on air defense, ballistic missile defense, and civil defense. Last June 18 the Soviets tested, apparently successfully, the command and control systems that would be required to make a nuclear surprise attack work. It seems clear enough to me, Mr. Chairman, that the Soviet leaders don't accept the MAD doctrine and never will. MAD is not a pact at all, just a one-way ticket to oblivion for the United States if we continue to cling to this preposterous doctrine.

"The practical reasons I have discussed are more than reason enough for us to abandon, once and for all, the doctrine of Mutual Assured Destruction, and to move in the direction that the President has pointed out for us. But there is for me an even more compelling reason:

"The MAD doctrine is immoral. There is something macabre, and worse, in basing our security on our ability to murder Russian women and children. And it is even more reprehensible—if that's possible—to deliberately increase the exposure of our own people to nuclear destruction simply in order to fulfill the demands of an abstract, a historical, unproven and illogical theory. We pray that deterrence will not fail. But if deterrence fails, there is nothing to be gained by massacring ordinary Russian civilians, the vast majority of whom have suffered more from Communism, and who hate Communism more than we ever will. Americans across the political spectrum have been uncomfortable with our strategic nuclear policy for some time, and I think the MAD doctrine is the reason why. Immoral policy is rarely ever good policy.

"By emphasizing strategic defense, President Reagan has pointed the way to a revised nuclear strategy that is logically sound and historically correct: that does not rely on the goodwill of the generals in the Kremlin to succeed, and which is based on the concept of saving lives, not destroying them.

"If we can create an effective ballistic missile defense, the American people no longer need fear a nuclear holocaust. We can lift that fear from the lives of all of our people without relying for our security on the goodwill and humanitarianism of leaders who have butchered innocents from Afghanistan to Poland, or on the promises of totalitarian leaders who have never kept such promises in the past.

"I should point out, in anticipation of objections which are sure to be raised, that an effective missile defense system need not be perfect in order to achieve a substantial reduction in danger.

"Furthermore, if we can create an effective ballistic missile defense, we can then begin to withdraw from our own arsenal the weapons of mass destruction that have cast such a pall over the world. If we can base our security on something more substantial than our ability to kill Russian women and children, we need no longer stockpile such weapons. We could take a very positive step toward reducing the number of offensive weapons in the world without fear of endangering our own security, and perhaps begin the process that would remove these nightmare weapons from the face of the earth.

"Experts assure me that it is both practicable and affordable for the United States to deploy an effective ballistic missile defense before the end of this century. I can think of no more worthy task than the one the President set before us on March 23rd. Let us get on with the task."[3]

At a Senate Armed Services Committee hearing on March 8, 1984, Senator Sam Nunn (D-Ga.) closely questioned several Defense Department officials on just what the SDI was expected to achieve. His most pointed questions concerned whether any defensive system could preclude the necessity of deploying offensive forces. All witnesses at this particular hearing seemed to agree that the United States could never abandon its offensive ICBM force. Following is part of the dialogue, from the March 8 hearing, among Nunn, Pentagon Research Chief Richard DeLauer, Director of the Defense Advanced Research Projects Agency Robert Cooper, and Undersecretary of Defense for Policy Fred Ikle.

Senator Nunn. [Dr. DeLauer,] I think I heard you say in the testimony, both in closed and in open sessions, and Dr. Ikle, too, as well as Dr. Cooper that one of the conceptual goals is to make Soviet offensive planning and attack more difficult.

Is that a fair assessment? . . .

Dr. DeLauer. Yes, sir, I think this will do that.

Senator Nunn. Another goal, as I understand it, is to preserve our capability to retaliate; in other words, the goal of being able to better protect our retaliatory capability?

Dr. DeLauer. Yes, sir. . . .

Senator Nunn. It would really protect any of our assets, bombers, missiles, submarines?

Dr. DeLauer. There is no question about that. With the effort we are doing in surveillance, that provides enough early warning in many situations to be able to handle our air-breathing assets, our bombers, by dispersion and by getting them off the fields.

Senator Nunn. . . . Would you say that it would be fair that this goal is also to avoid the necessity of threatening instant retaliation in response to a Soviet offensive threat?

Dr. DeLauer. The strategy for utilization of this force, I think, provides a better capability for . . . options.

If, indeed, it enhances the survivability of our assets, then it ought to provide . . . a greater degree of freedom and choice in utilization of these assets.

Senator Nunn. Can you envision our having a system that would avoid the necessity of deploying our offensive forces?

Dr. DeLauer. No.

Senator Nunn. Does anyone?

Dr. Ikle. Not in the foreseeable future. If you moved into an entirely different situation in the next century, where you would have a combination of agreement and defenses, that would be a different world.

Senator Nunn. One of the President's goals, as I understand it, in his initial thrust and speech was to avoid the necessity of having offensive retaliatory forces. It is a very attractive concept to say we can develop a defensive system that will avoid offensive forces on our side and perhaps even on their side.

Is that anywhere in the ballpark of what we are talking about?

Dr. Ikle. The President's statement focused on ballistic missiles and ballistic missile defenses. It still left open the air-breathing deterrent and air-breathing attack.

Senator Nunn. Let us confine it to offensive systems. Can anyone visualize in the next 25 years time frame that we will have good defensive capability if everything works out, and that we would then not have to rely on retaliation with offensive missiles ourselves? . . .

Dr. DeLauer. I can say within my lifetime I don't envision that nuclear weapons will be completely eliminated. Nevertheless, I believe that the research program we are proposing offers the promise of moving us toward a time when significantly reduced reliance on such weapons could be possible.

Dr. Cooper. I think it is fair to say that there is no combination of gold or platinum bullets that we see in our technology arsenal that we are pursuing in this program that would make it possible to do away with our strategic offensive ICBM forces.

Senator Nunn. I think that is clear.

Dr. Cooper. But, . . . there is a small percent of our program, about 5 percent of the dollars, that you will allocate that will be used to explore advanced concepts, a number of which were uncovered by the Fletcher committee, which could provide an entirely new silver bullet, which could make ballistic missiles irrelevant for the future. . . .

Dr. Ikle. Forty years ago there were no nuclear weapons. Things do change.

Senator Nunn. No doubt about it.

What the President said in his television speech was: "If free people could live in security and knowledge that security did not rest upon the threat of instant U.S. retaliation to deter Soviet attack, we would interdict and destroy strategic missiles before they reached our shores and our allies, would it not be better to save lives than avenge them?"

I certainly agree it would be much better to save lives than avenge them.

I don't think you are describing a program here that in any way diminishes the necessity of our retaliatory threat to avenge as well as to save. Are you?

Dr. DeLauer. We have argued that it is a deterrent. The minute you start talking about deployment. . .

Senator Nunn. The President was talking about what we have done when they have already fired, deterrence has not worked. He is talking about basically holding out to free people we are going to do away with the necessity of avenging, that is, retaliating.

I am trying to get the concept. If that is part of what we are talking about now, we ought to make it clear.

Dr. Ikle. Senator, things aren't black and white. There is often a mixture.

In the 1950s, which we all remember, we had substantial defensive capability and the time and ambition to make that defensive capability nearly perfect. Yet we relied on deterrent strikes of the Strategic Air Command.

Senator Nunn. Agreed.

Dr. Ikle. It reduced the likelihood of mass destruction. Yet, we have deterrence in a defensive system.

Senator Nunn. If everybody agrees we are talking about an 8- or 9-year program before we reach the point of decision-making, we are going to have to have support from this administration and the next administration, Democrat or Republican, liberals or conservatives, if this money we are spending, $24 or $25 billion, is not going to be just an empty dumping out of money.

You have to have a long-term program. The concept of where you are going is enormously important. If the American people believe they are supporting a program based on doing away with offensive weapons, which I think everybody has stipulated here will not happen in Dick DeLauer's time, that is one thing.

When they wake up and find out that is not what we are going to be doing—we will go for both offensive and defensive—they will have a change of heart.

I have not heard population protection mentioned anywhere in any of these presentations.

Are you talking about a system to protect populations and U.S. cities?

Dr. DeLauer. . . . What we are trying to do is enhance deterrence. If you enhance deterrence, and if your deterrence is credible and it holds, the people are protected.

Senator Nunn. That is also true of massive retaliation, that is a deterrent. Any deterrent system that prevents nuclear war will protect the population.

We are talking about systems where the deterrent has failed and missiles are flying.

Dr. DeLauer. . . . If you have a terminal defense, the chances of protecting everyone are limited.

If you have a midcourse defense system, then the question of consequences on the population depends on the leakage. But the chances for serious effects for intercepting and destroying nuclear warheads, even with salvage fusing, if done in the midcourse, the consequences on the ground are very, very small.

If you get them in the boost phase, the leakage is so much less that the end result is protection of the population.

Senator Nunn. I would agree with that to some extent. As you know, there is an enormous difference in designing systems to protect missile fields, bombers, and so forth, where you have 50-percent, even 30 to 40 percent survivability, and can then retaliate. . . .

It is a different thing when you are protecting a population where 30-percent leakage or 30-percent failure basically means 200 to 300 American cities at least are destroyed. . . .

You are describing possible collateral benefits as incidental to protecting populations.

Is that a fair assessment?

Dr. DeLauer. That is one consequence of a boost-phase defense system. I think it is unlikely at this stage of the game that I could give you a definitive answer.

Depending on the consequences of this program, the result can very well be that a deployment decision could indeed be for the purpose of preventing attack on cities and, therefore, populations.

I don't know. That is what we are going to find out. . . .

Senator Nunn. You are not sure now that will be a goal?

Dr. DeLauer. Only when we know the answer as to what we get.[4]

President Reagan commissioned two studies shortly after his March 1983 speech. One of these, the Hoffman Report, considered the strategic implications of the SDI. It has become one of the most often quoted sources favoring the deployment of space weaponry. The Hoffman Report is the result of work done by a team of scientists led by Mr. Fred Hoffman of Panheuristics, a California defense firm. The basic conclusions of the report are simple:

- The SDI would promote arms negotiations. This would be accomplished because the Soviets would not negotiate in good faith unless they knew the United States was firm and able to resist coercion. The SDI would demonstrate this firmness.
- The erosion of confidence within the Western alliance would be halted. The report argues that the erosion of confidence was caused by adverse shifts in the military balance. The SDI would change that.
- U.S. development and deployment of such a system would be necessary to counter a possible one-sided Soviet deployment. It was argued that this one-sided deployment could be quite near.
- Technologies for the SDI were advancing rapidly. An effective strategic defense would soon be possible.

The report also argued for the deployment of intermediate systems as they were developed. These interim systems would solve short-term security problems while the full system was being developed. "Fundamentally, the choice between the two paths depends on the utility of intermediate systems in meeting our national security objectives. In the discussion of ballistic missile defenses that preceded the U.S. proposal of the ABM Treaty, opponents of such defenses argued that the utility of widespread defense deployments should be judged in terms of their ability to protect population from large attacks aimed primarily at urban–industrial areas. Because of the destructiveness of nuclear weapons, nearly leakproof defenses are required to provide a high level of protection for population against such attacks. Moreover, opponents at that time also divided our strategic objectives into two categories: deterrence of war and limiting damage if deterrence failed. They relegated defenses exclusively to the second objective and ignored the essential complementarity between the two objectives. Consequently, they assigned defenses no role in deterrence.

"We have reexamined this issue, and we conclude that defenses of intermediate levels of capability can make critically important contributions to our national security objectives. *In particular, they can reinforce or help maintain deterrence by denying the Soviets confidence in their ability to achieve the strategic objectives of their contemplated attacks as they assess a decision to go to war.* By strengthening deterrence *at various levels of conflict,* defenses can also contribute valuable reassurance to our allies. . . .

"Soviet response to prospective or actual defense deployments by the United States also will have longer-run aspects. The Soviets' initial reaction will be to assess the nature, effects, and likelihood of a U.S. defense deployment. Barring fundamental changes in their conception of their relations to other states and their security needs, they will seek to prevent such a deployment through manipulation of public opinion or negotiations over arms agreements."[5]

In essence, the report was pessimistic about the present situation. Arms control was considered useless because the Soviets would not bargain in good faith under present circumstances. The Western alliance was seen as faltering because the United States was no longer in a position of being able to guarantee deterrence, owing to the Soviet weapons buildup. The study team predicted that the Soviets would try to capitalize on this rift in the alliance. Finally, the U.S. public, in the face of the massive Soviet arms buildup, seemed to be more fearful of war. These trends showed no sign of changing.

The only answer, the study team concluded, was a defensive strategy like the SDI. The SDI would restore the strategic balance, force the Soviets to negotiate in good faith, heal the problems within the Western alliance, and make the public less fearful of nuclear destruction.

When presented to Congress, the report was reviewed with skepticism by many senators and members of the House. Some thought the conclusions were rather simplistic. Floor debate and committee hearings brought out many other aspects of the problem of space weaponry that had to be considered.

Proponents of the SDI argued strongly that a strategic defense would indeed be a boon to arms reduction. Lt. General James Abrahamson, SDI director, claimed that the real value of such a system is that it reduces the military value of the large number of Soviet ballistic missiles. "As it reduces that military value," Abrahamson testified before the House Republican Study Committee, "it gives us more leverage, and I believe that leverage then becomes available to our arms control negotiations as a way to try to find ways to, in fact, remove the missiles themselves. So we cannot only have an effective defense, but we will be able to reduce the stockpile of ballistic missiles as a second step."[6]

Dr. Colin Gray, a member of the General Advisory Commission on Arms Control, went even further. He claimed that meaningful arms reductions would be impossible without such a defense system: "Today the addition of 20 or 30 ballistic or cruise missile warheads to the Soviet strategic arsenal is of no significance. But, if President Reagan's vision of a nuclear-disarmed world were to come to pass, solemnized and effected by a disarmament treaty, a Soviet Union that successfully hid 20 or 30, or perhaps even many less, nuclear weapons and their means of delivery, would have [on] hand the means for political intimidation for global hegemony. To be very blunt about it, the United States could sign a treaty for truly drastic reductions in the size of nuclear arsenals, let alone for zero-scale nuclear arsenals, only if it had in place a convincing array of active strategic defenses."[7]

Congressman Ken Kramer (R-Colo.) agreed with that assessment. Kramer noted that all agreements made so far had not brought about meaningful reductions in arms, and had not lowered the terrors nuclear war would bring: "The only way it will be possible to begin reducing nuclear arms stockpiles significantly to levels below the assured retaliation threshold, is that the United States and the U.S.S.R. can be reasonably certain that they have the means to offset such a reduction with a simultaneous deployment of non-nuclear defensive weapons, what I call strategic arms setoff, or STARS."[8]

Proponents of the SDI also point to its use as an option for dealing with smaller countries or terrorists. This argument claims that with the proliferation of nuclear technology, it is only a matter of time before countries like Iran, Libya, and others have the ability to create nuclear weapons. Terrorists could also get their hands on the materials and technology needed to create these weapons. Even if MAD continues to work for the United States and the Soviet Union, such a system of logical self-interest would be inapplicable to fanatical regimes or terrorist organizations. The only alternative would be a strategic defense.

Congressman Henry Hyde (R-Ill.) raised the issue of using strategic defenses for dealing with fanatics at a hearing of the House Foreign Affairs Subcommittee on International Security and Scientific Affairs in questions directed to Dr. Kurt Gottfried of the Union of Concerned Scientists.

Dr. Gottfried. The question we have to ask ourselves is, what is the consequence of SDI for United States–Soviet political and military relationships? I personally feel that this business of shifting the argument to what we are going to do about Qadhafi and

Khomeini and Qadhafi-primed and unborn Qadhafis is simply not serious because surely if Mr. Qadhafi wants to do something to us, he will send it on a boat—or by suitcase—and it will arrive right here, maybe, in the basement of this building, and you will get a phone call that there is a bomb there. It is not going to come with an intercontinental ballistic missile from Libya.

Mr. Hyde. No; I tend to agree with you, but we focus so much on Soviet–American relationships that I do think that the day isn't long when this weapon, whether it is brought in a suitcase or fabricated over here and not brought in, is a more likely problem.[9]

Those representing the viewpoint of Congressman Hyde tend to worry more about the future of nuclear proliferation and the tendency that a nuclear disaster, if it occurred, would most likely not be a U.S.–Soviet conflict. Dr. Gottfried's point—that it would not make sense to spend hundreds of billions of dollars on an undefined future threat—is the most common response. Others argue that rather than enhancing arms control, such a defense might increase the chance of nuclear war.

The problem lies in the fact that this defense would not be a "perfect" defense. Although the final goal is a defense that would "make nuclear weapons obsolete," no one would argue that the defense would, from day one, be impenetrable. The Senate Foreign Relations Committee looked at this problem in a hearing on April 25, 1984.

Senator Pressler. How do you respond to the argument that if strategic defense is going to make us a little safer, why not build it? If it makes us two percent safer, why not build it? If it makes us 10 percent safer, why not build it? That is what people say to me when I say we should negotiate first . . . although I do support research during the interim.

Dr. Albert Carnesale [Harvard University]. The ability to intercept 2 or 5 percent of Soviet RVs does not make us 2 or 5 percent safer. Indeed, if such a defense made it more likely that they would launch an attack, it would have made us less safe than we were before. . . .

Dr. Sidney D. Drell [Stanford University]. If I thought that we would have a safer world by a path like this, I would indeed support it. The problem is that as a unilateral initiative . . . based upon a decision taken unilaterally by the United States, we have to ask how will the Soviets react or how would we react if the Soviets did the same thing, and will this contribute to making the world safer.

Permit me to read a short quotation from a former President of the United States who faced this decision in 1969 when he decided not to build a nationwide defense, and when he announced it to the nation. It was a statement by President Nixon: "Although every instinct motivates me to provide the American people with complete protection against a major nuclear attack, it is not now within our power to do so." I think you heard this morning that this is still a true statement. It is not now within our power to do so. "The heaviest defense system we considered," the quote goes on, "one designed to protect our major cities still could not prevent a catastrophic level of U.S. fatalities from a deliberate, all-out Soviet attack."

Again, that is a statement that we have heard since President Eisenhower. It is the nature of nuclear weapons and their enormous destructive power that if even one lands on a city, that is the end of the city. But then, the key sentence of President Nixon's speech on March 14, 1969—"and it might look to an opponent like the prelude to an offensive strategy threatening the Soviet deterrent."

I think that is the problem. Without arms control restraints, a unilateral change in the fundamental strategic relation, going for defenses at the same time as we are strengthening our offense, faces them with a view we would like no more if we saw it coming at us: namely, a major enhancement of offensive forces to preserve the retaliatory or deterrent capability, and at the same time, a defense which, as an adjunct of a first strike, would have to handle only a surviving retaliatory force—drizzle instead of a downpour coming back—and could be more effective. And that is the problem. It is destabilizing.[10]

This argument by Dr. Drell added a new twist. Although most U.S. citizens do not expect that we would strike first in a nuclear war, the Soviets are not so sure. If this type of a system would be much more effective in a first-strike situation, the Soviets could see the act of building a strategic defense as provocative. This could lead to a preemptive Soviet attack. By this analysis, such a defensive system could increase rather than decrease the chances of nuclear war.

Lt. General James Abrahamson was questioned on this:

[*Representative Dan Burton* (R-Ind.).] General, . . . I wonder how you would respond to those critics of the SDI who say that this will take us to the brink of war.

General Abrahamson. My first response is I don't understand why.

Mr. Burton. Well, neither do I, but that question arises on the Floor of the House all the time.

General Abrahamson. I believe that the real problem is, that very often, they are using some slogan to simplify what is really a very complex kind of deterrent equation. In fact, in a discussion with a representative of the Soviet Union, he put it to me that way.

He said, "It is clear that if one side developed a thoroughly effective system and the other side had none, that would be a dangerous imbalance." If that were the Soviet Union and we had none on the other side, I don't think that we would ever initiate a preemptive attack on the other side. . . .

If we were going to be able to develop this and have it all be put in place at 12 o'clock noon on June 30th in 1995, then yes, there probably is a danger that at 11:58 somebody might be inclined to say, "I have to stop this."

But that isn't the way we do things in this country, and that isn't the way this will develop. It will develop, as I say, incrementally over time. As it develops, I believe that the Soviet Union . . . will continue to work in the same direction.[11]

Senator Paul Tsongas (D-Mass.) tried a different approach during a hearing of the Senate Foreign Relations Committee. He asked Assistant Secretary of Defense Richard Perle whether we would be compelled to shoot down a Soviet system, if they were to develop and attempt to deploy a strategic defense system. Perle responded that he did not know, that such a scenario would present "a very difficult policy question," and that "we do not believe that such a move by the Soviet Union is imminent."[12]

General James Abrahamson also dismissed the question, saying that "in real life, we would see, long before they deployed such a system, evidence that they were working on it, and indeed that is the case."[13]

Many argue that rather than attacking us—which would in any case be suicide for the Soviets—they would simply go full speed at building their own defensive system. That would be, in effect, what the president wants. That also would be in line with the argument of General Abrahamson that such developments would occur incrementally. Each side could assess the advances of the other. Both sides would therefore advance incrementally to develop defensive systems. With both defensive systems intact, nuclear weapons would be less useful. Then arms reductions could begin.

This viewpoint is also not without criticism. Dr. Albert Carnesale of Harvard University, in testimony before the Senate Foreign Relations Committee, offered a scenario in which both sides had a reasonably effective space-based strategic defense. Dr. Carnesale drew the logical conclusion that if they could destroy ballistic missiles, they could destroy satellites as well. Satellites would be easier targets. In other words, the defensive systems could destroy each other.

Dr. Carnesale. Now think of the incentive to go first. By attacking the other fellow's "Star Wars" satellites, you accomplish two things simultaneously. First, his nation is now vulnerable to your offensive missiles, because you have destroyed his defense; and second, your nation remains invulnerable to his offensive systems, because you have retained your defense. So if these things work, I can think of nothing less stable than for both countries to have them simultaneously.

Senator Tsongas. So, as to the desirability of first strike, it is the function of how effective a system is?

Dr. Carnesale. It is a function of how effective it is, but if it is reasonably effective, as the proponents would have us believe, then it maximizes the incentive on both sides. Imagine what would happen if you were struck first. You would suddenly find yourself in a situation where you were vulnerable to his offensive weapons and he was not vulnerable to yours.

This is a situation in which I would not like to find us. This is a situation in which the Soviets would not like to find themselves. For both sides to have space-based defenses would be the worst of all situations.[14]

This argument directly confronts the argument of SDI proponents that possession of a strategic defense system by both sides would remove the threat of war. Ironically, this analysis suggests that the more effective the defense, the greater will be the threat of war.

There are also strategic implications tied directly to the mechanics of the system itself. For the defense to be highly effective, missiles must be attacked while they are in their "boost phase" or in the "bus phase" prior to release of warheads and decoys. The boost phase occurs during a three- to five-minute period after launch, while the missiles are gaining speed and before the release of individual warheads. In order to stop the missiles in this phase, defensive systems need to be activated almost immediately. Once the warheads are released, the chances are much greater that they could overwhelm the defense. It would be virtually impossible for the president or other high-echelon officials to approve the activation of defense systems that would require almost instantaneous response, thus diminishing the vital human decision-making element. Computers would make the defenses operative at the split second that missile launchings were detected.

Dr. George Keyworth, President Reagan's science advisor, in response to a question from Senate Foreign Relations Committee Chairman Charles Percy (R-Ill.), dismissed the possibility of a defense system shooting down nonmilitary spacecraft: "I think the example of shooting down a spacecraft is to pay little attention to the immense progress in technology that is occurring. You simply must develop a system where that opportunity is negligibly small."[15]

Senator Percy was not completely satisfied with that answer and pressed the president's science advisor for more details:

The Chairman. We have had an alarming number of documented computer failures at the North American Air Defense Command (NORAD). I happened to be there years ago, visiting with a group of business people, and . . . a false signal actually came in.

A national publication later described that incident, and none of us could even recognize the chaos and confusion that we saw with our own eyes as against the article which portrayed it as an incident that we could somehow handle.

Would you be comfortable in taking men completely out of the decision loop in view of the number of alarming false signals that we have had at NORAD? Isn't there just too great a probability of our initiating hostilities by error?

Dr. Keyworth. The reason why, in spite of a number of glitches over the years, as you have described, we have not yet had any disastrous consequences in terms of initiating a nuclear exchange, is because we have built in so many, many cross-checks and mechanisms to prevent that.

Clearly, in this system, the same thing would have to be done. We have a vast capability today, technological capability, that we did not possess ten, let alone twenty years ago. I believe that the system could be made absolutely safe. But I especially emphasize here that we are not talking about the initiation of a nuclear exchange, and that is the very stabilizing result that we are trying to achieve by introducing defense into our strategic posture to remove the threat of initiating nuclear war.

What we are talking about is defending against an attack against the United States.

The Chairman. Well, putting it another way, taking into account the state of the art now and what we contemplate as the state of the art: . . . Would you sleep well at night knowing that we have put all our eggs in one basket and that we had delegated responsibility for strategic deterrence to computers, actually?

What if our self-contained space defense system were to fail to respond to an actual Soviet attack? Could we trust it not to do so really?

Dr. Keyworth. Senator, none of us has ever proposed, nor do I think any of us believe that we are describing or discussing here some magical shield under which we can live with no concerns. We are talking about an element of our defense posture and a gradual change in strategy, a strategy in which ultimately the Strategic Defense Initiative will be one single component. To focus just upon the Strategic Defense Initiative I do not believe you will have man completely out of the loop. You will have a decision that will have to be made in a compressed period of time. Therefore, data processing will play a very high role.[16]

At the same hearing, Dr. Robert Cooper, director of the Defense Advanced Research Projects Agency, explained how human decision making could be involved despite boost-phase time constraints: "It could be possible that if tensions had risen and we were at DEFCON 4 or 5, that the President would be available and could make decisions on a few-minute time scale. . . . No one knows exactly what the system design would be or what technology it would employ to put the command and control authorities into a position where they could start and stop the system."[17] Dr. Cooper alluded to the Safeguard system of the late 1960s, which, using computers of that time, performed similar chores of detecting and responding to any possible Soviet attack. The system could be either started or stopped, and would have been started only in a time of extreme tension. The SDI, Dr. Cooper pointed out, would not be using computers of the 1960s, but would comprise technology from the 1990s or later.

An intense exchange clearly demonstrated the arguments on both sides of this concern:

Senator Tsongas [(D-Mass.)]. Has the President been informed that he is out of the decisionmaking loop?

General Abrahamson. Sir, we have not defined this whole program yet. I think that is a key and important point.

Senator Tsongas [to Dr. Keyworth]. Have you said to him, "Mr. President, the likelihood is, if there is not tension so that we know it is coming . . . that if there were a strike, the fact is you are not in the decisionmaking process."

Dr. Keyworth. I certainly have not. (Laughter.) Senator, I think we are obscuring the central point. This is not an analogy with initiating a war or carrying out a war. It may very well be nothing more than sending a few beams of light out into space. No one is to be injured. . . . The President is perfectly clear of the exact time sequence you have asked. We have made that clear to him. He understands it perfectly. You are asking for a decision that is not an analog to the nuclear launch decision. It is a totally different situation. . . .

Mr. Perle. May I add something?

Senator Tsongas. Have you told him, Mr. Perle? Are you the one who had the duty of telling him that he is not part of the process?

Mr. Perle. Senator, I have to say that I do not understand your concern, and I would like to understand your concern. You are hypothesizing a situation in which a nuclear attack is launched on the United States, in which hundreds or perhaps thousands of nuclear warheads are headed for the destruction of our homeland, and you are worried about whether the President is going to make a decision to intercept those incoming warheads.

Frankly, I think the question of Presidential intervention or any other intervention is a minor, second-order issue when the real issue is whether you do or do not stop the destruction of the United States.

Senator Tsongas. How does the President feel about your viewing him as a minor, second-order level of decisionmaking?

Mr. Perle. I said the decision is a minor decision because it does no harm if it turns out there is not an attack, and if there is an attack. . .

Senator Tsongas. Mr. Perle, some of us believe that a nuclear war is not a minor decision. And to describe that as a minor decision suggests why there is such a gulf between those of you at that table and some of us up here.

Mr. Perle. I think you have distorted the clear intent of what I have said.[18]

Senator Joseph Biden (D-Del.) also joined the debate. He questioned both General Abrahamson and Mr. Perle about the possibility that either (1) the U.S. system might shoot down a Soviet spacecraft or (2) if activated in error, the Soviets might read it as a beginning of hostilities.

In response to the first possibility, Mr. Perle claimed that the launching of spacecraft and ICBMs was different. A spacecraft has a different trajectory than a missile, Perle stated, and the U.S. defense system would be required to discriminate among trajectories.

To Senator Biden's second concern, Mr. Perle denied that the Soviets would overreact to a mistake on our part. "The Soviets would know that their satellites have not come under attack. They would know that."[19]

Senator Biden responded, "But you do not think they would conclude anything else? You think they would conclude that it is a mistake? You do not think they would think that they were in fact under attack and we just blew it, that we missed it, which means they better do something?"[20]

One conclusion is obvious from the above debate: Many problems with the SDI had not yet been solved. Administration witnesses frequently noted that problems raised by senators were still being researched, and that future technologies would be able to handle many of these problems. Indeed, it is impossible for such problems to be worked out at this early stage.

10

Technology

This chapter highlights the various reports on the state of SDI technology and the often lively debate in Congress concerning this crucial issue.

Congress had heard testimony from individuals and aerospace companies that advocated space-based defenses as early as 1982, months before President Reagan called for the SDI. The best known of these early space-based defense concepts was Lt. General Daniel Graham's High Frontier proposal. High Frontier would use existing, "off-the-shelf" technology for quick deployment of space-based defenses.

High Frontier was to be built with current technology instead of futuristic beam weapons. Its advocates said costs could be kept to $15 billion. When the Pentagon first reviewed the proposal, it concluded that High Frontier could cost between $200 and $300 billion. In time, the Defense Department revised this estimate downward somewhat, but not before Congress had heard much conflicting testimony.

General Graham, former director of the Defense Intelligence Agency, described his High Frontier concept at a Senate Foreign Relations Committee hearing on April 14, 1983: "I should point out that the High Frontier system . . . does not employ lasers and does not employ particle beam weapons or any futuristic Buck Rogers system. In fact, High Frontier uses kinetic energy kill; that is, a kill of the Soviet weapons with pellets, like buckshot.

"If you worry that this is not technically feasible, I would like to call your attention and the attention of your staffs to a document recently declassified by the Department of Defense which was Project Defender. In Project Defender, in 1962, 20 of the best scientists within the Department of Defense, backed by a staff of 5,000 technicians and administrative personnel, came to the conclusion that a defense such as High Frontier's could have been deployed by 1968.

"So we are not talking Buck Rogers when we back the President's call for a defense in space. We do not have to have lasers or particle beam weapons, although High Frontier has no objections to such weapons and a second generation may include them. The fact of the matter is that within 5 or 6 years, at a cost not of many billions but of $15 billion, a strategic defense can be had by this country. If President Reagan runs again, he may see a space-borne defense against the long-range Soviet ballistic missiles during the period of his Presidency."[1]

Interestingly, Dr. Edward Teller, a leading advocate of the SDI, was not supportive of High Frontier. At a Senate Armed Services Committee hearing on May 2, 1983, Dr. Teller said, in part, "I greatly prefer a world where all sides are armed with shields to a world where all sides are armed with swords and no shields. I believe that the emphasis on defense can lessen the inherent probability of war.

"I might add that I had the pleasure to participate in the High Frontier effort. I agree fully with that emphasis on defense. I agree with the emphasis on speed. I fully agree with the emphasis on space.

"But I could not agree on the technical execution. . . . We need a strong defense. But $100 billion expended on this effort of defense the Soviets would counter by a few billion dollars in offense.

"For that reason, having attended the meeting on High Frontier, I most regretfully was unable to sign the final document."[2]

At a Senate Foreign Relations Committee hearing on September 20, 1982,[3] both Robert Cooper and Richard DeLauer stated that the Pentagon was not seriously considering the High Frontier concept. Cooper added, "The enormous complexity of such a system is unmanageable today, in our judgment, and we need basic . . . breakthroughs in the ability to manage large complex systems before any such system might be feasible in the future."

President Reagan, by contrast to the off-the-shelf technology of High Frontier, challenged U.S. scientists to cross new frontiers in space by devising some of the most exotic weapons and deployment systems ever visualized.

Shortly after his March 1983 speech, Mr. Reagan commissioned two studies: one on the prospects for developing antimissile defenses and the other on the strategic ramifications of such a new defense policy. Findings of the first panel, the Defense Technologies Study Team, became known as the Fletcher Report, after Chairman

James C. Fletcher, former National Aeronautics and Space Administration administrator and later professor of engineering and technology at the University of Pittsburgh. Findings of the second panel, the Future Security Strategy Study Team, became known as the Hoffman Report after Chairman Fred S. Hoffman of the California defense firm, Panheuristics.

The two teams reported to the president in the fall of 1983. Unclassified summaries of both reports were provided to the Senate Foreign Relations Committee at an April 25, 1984, hearing by Lt. General James A. Abrahamson, SDI Office director.

In its report to Congress on the SDI in 1985, the Department of Defense reiterated its support for the findings of the Fletcher study as the theoretical basis for research. The report elaborated on, but did not depart from, the principles set forth in the unclassified summary of the Fletcher study presented to Congress by General Abrahamson.

These were among the conclusions reached by Fletcher's Defensive Technologies Study Team:

- Powerful technologies are becoming available that justify a major technology development effort offering future technical options to implement a defensive strategy.
- Focused development of technologies for a comprehensive BMD will require strong central management.
- The most effective systems have multiple layers, or tiers.
- Survivability of the system components is a critical issue whose resolution requires a combination of technologies and tactics that remain to be worked out.
- Significant demonstrations of developing technologies for critical BMD functions can be performed over the next ten years that will provide visible evidence of progress in developing the technical capabilities required of an effective in-depth defense system.[4]

The unclassified summary of the Fletcher Report concluded on an optimistic note: "The technological challenges of a strategic defense initiative are great but not insurmountable. By pursuing the long-term, technically feasible research and development plan identified by the Study Team and presented in this report, the United States will reach that point where knowledgeable decisions concerning an engineering validation phase can be made with confidence. The scientific community may indeed give the United States 'the means of rendering' the ballistic missile threat 'impotent and obsolete'."[5]

Specific provisions of the report worth noting here are included in the following excerpts: "The four phases of a typical ballistic missile trajectory are: . . . First, . . . a boost phase when the first- and second-stage engines are burning and offering intense, highly specific observables. A post-boost, or bus deployment, phase occurs next, during which multiple warheads and penetration aids are released from a post-boost vehicle. Then, there is a midcourse phase when warheads and penetration aids travel on ballistic trajectories above the atmosphere. Finally, there is a terminal phase in which the warheads and penetration aids reenter the atmosphere and are affected by atmospheric drag. . . .

"It is generally accepted, on the basis of many years of ballistic missile defense studies and associated experiments, that an efficient defense against a high-level threat would be a multitiered defense-in-depth. . . . For each tier there will be leakage, that is, threat objects that have not been intercepted and hence move on to the next phase. For example, three tiers, each of which allows 10 percent leakage, yielding an overall leakage of 0.1 percent, are likely to be less costly than a single layer that is 99.9 percent effective. In addition, a multitiered defense is the optimum counter to structured attacks: any given offense response affects only one phase. . . .

"The phenomenology and required technology for each of these phases of a ballistic missile trajectory are quite different. In each phase of a ballistic missile flight, a defensive system must perform the basic functions of (1) surveillance, acquisition, and tracking and (2) intercept and target destruction. . . .

"The surveillance, acquisition, and tracking function includes sensing information for battle management and processing signals and data for discrimination of threatening reentry vehicles from other objects. As each potential reentry vehicle is released from its post-boost vehicle, it begins ballistic midcourse flight accompanied by deployment hardware and possibly by decoys. Each credible object must be accounted for in a birth-to-death track, even if the price is many decoy false alarms. Interceptor vehicles of the defense must also be tracked."

INTERCEPT AND TARGET DESTRUCTION

"A variety of mechanisms, including directed energy, can destroy a target at any point along its trajectory. The study identified several promising ones. An excimer laser, for example, can be configured to produce a single giant pulse that delivers a resulting shock wave to a target. The shock causes structural collapse. A continuous-wave or repetitively pulsed laser delivers radiant thermal energy to the target.

Contact is maintained until a hole is burned through the target or the temperature of the entire target is raised to a damaging level. Examples included in this category are free-electron lasers, chemical lasers (hydrogen fluoride or deuterium fluoride), and repetitively pulsed excimer lasers. Another way to destroy a target is with a neutral-particle beam, which deposits sufficient energy within a target to destroy its internal components. Guns and missiles destroy their targets through kinetic-energy impact. Here, homing projectiles are propelled by chemical rockets or by hypervelocity guns, such as the electromagnetic gun based on the idea of an open solenoid."

BATTLE MANAGEMENT

"The purpose of battle management is to optimize the use of defense resources—it is a data-processing and communication system that includes the command, control, and communication facilities. Its tasks are situation monitoring, resource accounting, resource allocation, and reporting.

"A layered battle-management system would correspond to the different layers of the ballistic missile defense system, with each layer being semiautonomous with its own processing resources, rules of engagement, sensor inputs, and weapons. During an engagement, data would be handed over from one phase to the next. Its exact architecture would be highly dependent on the mix of sensors and weapons and the geographical scope of the defensive system that it manages. . . .

"There are several critical technological issues that will probably require research programs of 10 to 20 years.

- *Boost and post-boost phases.* As mentioned earlier, the ability to effectively respond to an unconstrained threat is strongly dependent on meeting it appropriately during the boost and bus deployment, or post-boost, phases. This is especially important for a responsive threat.
- *Threat clouds.* Large threat clouds—that is, dense concentrations of reentry vehicles, decoys, and debris in great numbers—must be identified and sorted out during the midcourse phase and high reentry.
- *Survivability.* It will be necessary to develop a combination of tactics and mechanisms ensuring the survival of the system's space-based components.
- *Interceptors.* By having inexpensive interceptors in the midcourse phase and in early reentry, intercept can be economical enough to permit attacks on threat objects that cannot be discriminated.

- *Battle Management.* Tools are needed for developing battle-management software."[6]

Dr. Sidney D. Drell, deputy director of the Stanford Linear Accelerator, evaluated the concept of a BMD defense at the April 25, 1984, hearing. These excerpts from his prepared statement sharply attack the conclusions presented by the Fletcher Report. "There have indeed been tremendous advances in recent years in the technology pertinent to this problem that have removed some of the shortcomings of previous defense concepts. These include producing directed-energy beams of high power that travel as accurate bullets at the speed of light, and more efficient gathering, processing and transmitting of vast quantities of data for the purpose of battle management. There have also been major improvements in the offensive forces. I have concluded, based on long experience and recent intense work on this problem, that we do not know how to build an effective nationwide defense, nor is there any prospect of achieving one in the foreseeable future, unless the offensive threat is first tightly constrained technically and greatly reduced numerically as a result of major progress in arms control. . . .

"The major technical fact that has not changed with time is the overwhelming destructive power of nuclear weapons. To speak, as President Reagan did, of rendering nuclear weapons 'impotent and obsolete' by defending one's vital national interests—people, industries, cities—against a massive nuclear attack still requires a defense that is almost perfect. Technical assessments of ABM concepts cannot escape this awesome systems requirement. If but 1 percent of the approximately 8,000 nuclear warheads on the current Soviet force of land-based and sea-based ballistic missiles succeeded in penetrating a defensive shield and landed on urban targets in the United States, it would be one of the greatest disasters in all history! . . .

". . . Even if the very ambitious and costly R&D program recently proposed by the Administration achieves all of its major goals, far beyond presently demonstrated technologies, great operational barriers will still remain. . . .

"As one looks at each layer of this defense, one encounters problems of monumental magnitude. In order to illustrate some of them I will describe the possibility of boost-phase intercept. It is the principal new element in considering ABM technologies. It also has the highest potential payoff for two reasons:

"1. Whatever success is achieved in this initial layer of the defense reduces the size of the attacking force to be engaged by each subsequent layer.

"2. If a missile is destroyed during boost when it is relatively vulnerable, all of its warheads and decoys are destroyed with it.

"Following the missile boost phase, the defense has more time for performing its functions of acquiring and discriminating warheads from decoys, attacking its targets and confirming their destruction. On the other hand, although not so severely constrained by very short engagement times, it must also cope with many more objects since a single large booster is capable of deploying tens of warheads and many hundreds of decoys. Thus the two defensive layers for boost-phase and for midcourse intercept face very different technological challenges. Moreover an effective boost-phase layer which greatly reduces the number of objects that subsequent layers must analyze and attack is crucial to overall effectiveness of a defensive system."

CHEMICAL LASERS BASED IN SPACE

"One of the most widely discussed systems for boost-phase intercept is a constellation of very high-powered chemical lasers and large optical systems operating to near-perfection that orbit the Earth in space. Very well focused laser beams have the attractive feature . . . of traveling vast distances with the speed of light in space above the atmosphere. The disadvantages of space-based lasers are that they are complex and expensive and vulnerable to direct attack. . . . Most simply, the space stations can be destroyed by relatively cheap space mines placed in nearby orbits and detonated by radio command from ground. Indeed the space stations themselves are more vulnerable than the ICBMs against which they are targeted. A space-based laser system does not offer a credible prospect of an effective defensive layer."

A 'POP-UP' SYSTEM OF X-RAY LASERS

"In order to avoid the vulnerability of space basing, the battle-stations may be mounted on a missile based on ground poised to launch—i.e. to 'pop up'—upon receipt of notification of enemy attack. The most promising 'pop-up' system of this type is an X-ray laser pumped by a nuclear explosion and designed to destroy attacking missiles during boost phase. . . .

"In considering the possibility of a practical 'pop-up' system of this type, the most difficult and important operational issue to address is if it can be launched sufficiently rapidly even to attempt a boost-phase intercept. . . . This means that the X-ray lasers have only 3–5 minutes in which to do their launch. However, X-rays are absorbed by the atmosphere, and so such a defensive system must itself reach an altitude well above 100 miles within that same short time interval in order to be able to shoot at the attacking missile. Furthermore, it would have to be based far off-shore near to Soviet territory. Otherwise, due to curvature of the Earth, it will be impossible for the X-ray laser beams to 'see' the booster above the horizon before the end of burn. . . .

"Other technologies and systems concepts have been proposed in an effort to escape the drawbacks of space-based and 'pop-up' systems. One such concept is that of a system of ground-based lasers whose beams are aimed up to a small number of large relay mirrors at high altitudes, in or near synchronous orbits at 40,000 km altitude. . . . This hybrid system . . . must conquer severe technological obstacles of transmitting its light through the atmosphere without loss of focussing due to atmospheric turbulence and without loss of energy due to absorption. . . . The few large focussing mirrors in space are themselves a small number of high-value and expensive targets vulnerable to attack. . . .

"Technologies other than laser beams are even less far along as candidates for ABM systems. Particle-beam technology is the least mature of the directed-energy technology efforts. . . .

"The data-handling—or battle management—problem is thought by many to represent the most stressing technological problem, and it is not fully understood at present.

"On top of all these problems, the entire system with its many hundreds of advanced sensors and interceptors, and its severe battle management requirements, would have to work to almost 100 percent perfection the first time it was used—although never fully tested under realistic conditions in the midst of nuclear explosions!"[7]

OTA was also pessimistic about the technological feasibility of a total missile defense. Its report, released in April 1984, was prepared at the request of Senators Pressler and Tsongas. It was drafted for OTA by Dr. Ashton B. Carter, a research fellow at the Massachusetts Institute of Technology's Center for International Studies. The report concluded: "The prospects that emerging 'Star Wars' technologies, when further developed, will provide a perfect or near-perfect defense system, literally removing from the hands of the Soviet Union the ability to do socially mortal damage to the United States with nuclear weapons, is so remote that it should not serve as the basis of public expectation or national policy about ballistic missile defense (BMD). This judgment appears to be the consensus among informed members of the defense technical community."[8]

These were among other significant, and controversial, judgments in the report:

- An imperfect defense would permit the Soviet Union to destroy the United States in a "massive attack," but might negate the effectiveness of "smaller, specialized nuclear strikes."
- Weapons needed for boost-phase intercept of ICBMs, a crucial element of the SDI, have not yet been built.
- A BMD system would be vulnerable to Soviet attack and would be susceptible to Soviet countermeasures.
- Present missile defenses present less technical risk than would systems stressing a boost-phase attack.
- The SDI is on a collision course with the ABM treaty, which prohibits deployment of missile defenses based on new technologies.

The OTA report so rankled the Pentagon that SDI Office Director Abrahamson submitted a strongly worded rebuttal to the Senate Foreign Relations Committee on May 8, 1984. In his statement, Abrahamson complained, "[The OTA] paper actually addresses neither the goals nor the merits of the SDI research program. Furthermore, independent authorities have found that the paper contains technical errors, unsubstantiated assumptions, and conclusions that are inconsistent with the analysis in the body of the report.

"It is basic to any assessment of the Strategic Defense Initiative to evaluate it as a research program exploring technologies that are not intended to be exploited for many years. Yet the paper challenges the SDI based on the capability of current defense technologies to counter offensive capabilities that are at least 20 years in the future. It also misleads the reader concerning the goals of the current research program, which are to provide future leaders with options for decisions they may have to make to strengthen deterrence with effective strategic defenses.

"While the body of the report repeatedly stresses the importance of a vigorous research and technology program as a hedge against unilateral Soviet exploitation of new technologies, the conclusions do not address the consequences of current and possible future Soviet efforts. It fails to consider the conclusions of the large body of national security experts who have studied the strategic implications of the SDI and judge that it can have great promise for strengthening deterrence and enhancing stability."[9]

OTA immediately submitted its report for review to three independent specialists: Dr. William Perry, former Pentagon research and engineering chief; Dr. Charles Townes, a Nobel Prize recipient and key advisor to Defense Secretary Weinberger; and Lt. General Glenn Kent, a retired air force general specializing in research and engineering. These experts supported the conclusions of the OTA report. On May 17, 1984, OTA provided the Senate Foreign Relations Committee with a point-by-point response to technical challenges posed by Abrahamson. OTA noted that its original paper on missile defense had stressed a fundamental distinction between useful but less-than-perfect defenses and defenses so perfect the Soviet Union could not destroy U.S. society with nuclear weapons. It concluded: "Insofar as the SDI aims at a perfect defense, the Background Paper casts doubt upon how realistic the program is. With respect to less-than-perfect defense, and with respect to ballistic missile defense in general, the Background Paper makes no judgments; it is at that point intended to be a technical primer on boost phase intercept technology. The Background Paper does not say that boost phase defense will not work at all, nor that less-than-perfect defenses are undesirable."[10]

In the early stages of the SDI debate, the questions most often asked of the experts by members of Congress were the following: How close are we to a SDI defense? Once deployed, how much protection would an SDI system actually provide?

Despite the optimistic note of his letter accompanying the Fletcher Report to Congress, Pentagon Research Chief Richard DeLauer answered the first question cautiously. An early deployment of an SDI defense is not in the cards, he said.

DeLauer testified on SDI technology at a November 10, 1983, hearing of the House Armed Services Subcommittee on Research and Engineering, which was considering the People Protection Act. "There's been a lot of loose talk to the effect that all we have to do is go out and do another Manhattan project or do another Apollo project and we've got this thing all straightened out.

"Just for clarity and completeness, remember that the Manhattan project had one purpose, create a device. They didn't have to worry about how they delivered it, that was already there. They didn't have to worry about the force structure that it took to deliver it, that was already there. They only had to create a device that worked and there was really only about two areas of technical uncertainty that had to be developed, and they went ahead and developed that. . . .

"The Apollo program had an infrastructure that existed out of the ballistic missile program. We knew how to build pumps, turbo-pumps. We knew how to build thrust chambers. We had to make them bigger, but we knew how to do the job. We had built guidance systems for the ballistic missiles that had every bit of capability to handle the Apollo mission. . . .

"Now as far as the implementation of the Apollo program was concerned, [this was] performed in a benign environment, not a hostile environment. This made the job much easier.

"The force structure consisted of Buzz Aldrin and his buddies. A finite number . . . So that's all they had to do was go get seven good guys and they had essentially their force structure. . . .

"Every single one of those areas of [SDI] technology has greater complexity than the programs that have been loosely talked about when people say that all we've got to do is go emulate what we did before.

"The last function, the battle management, is probably the most awesome. To be able to do all the things that we have to do we must accomplish discrimination, command, control and damage assessment. You've got to know whether we can do many things that we can't do yet. . . . We don't have the computers, we don't have the capability of hardening things against countermeasures."[11]

At a Senate Foreign Relations Committee hearing on April 25, 1984, Senator John Glenn (D-Ohio) complained that the technology for a multilayer missile defense "has not yet been invented" but that the public was being led to believe such a system could be deployed immediately. "I have followed all the different types of lasers, high velocity kinetic weapons, particle beams, and such for I guess about 15 or 18 years now. . . .

"I have supported laser research and particle beam research for ground use and for battlefield use and so on in the thought that perhaps it might have some application in the future, perhaps in space, too. But it seemed to me ever since the President has talked about this that what we are talking about is something that has not yet been invented. While I support research, all this business of going on with proposals for deployment and such are so premature at this point that I cannot believe we are discussing layers 1 through 5 and are just assuming that the basic physics of this thing works. That is a long way from being proven.

"It may be another 15 or 20 years before we have the thing workable.

"I just can't see this. The President far oversold this. I thought it started for political reasons. If he wants to appear to be Buck Rogers out there, defending the country, that is fine. I appreciate that. But I just cannot see us going through all this business of deployment, having great teams going out, doing decision-making and all of that business when the basic system has not even been invented."[12]

Glenn, the first American to orbit the Earth, also took issue with experts who compared the SDI with the Apollo project. Apollo, he said, was an engineering problem, while Star Wars will require "some very basic technological breakthroughs." He asserted, "I think the whole idea of going ahead and spending a lot of money is foolish. Secretary DeLauer said to me that maybe his estimates are that it could be as much as eight times the Apollo program in expense and could cost up to a trillion dollars. Why go ahead planning now to deploy this thing before the whole thing has even been invented?"[13]

Dr. Robert Cooper, director of the Defense Advanced Research Projects Agency, and Dr. George A. Keyworth, President Reagan's science advisor, agreed with some of Glenn's observations, while Richard Perle, assistant secretary of defense, took issue with the senator's statements. Following are excerpts from the exchange between Glenn and these experts at the April 25, 1984, hearing:

Dr. Cooper. Senator, you are exactly right, and I agree with you 100 percent—that is, we are talking about technology which is not mature. All this program has been represented as, both by the President and the Defense Department, is as a research and development program to bring the technology which might be applied in this area to maturity.

We have estimated 10 to 20 years to do that.

I agree with you that it is not an engineering problem. There are some basic and fundamental things that we need to develop, particularly in the data processing area.

Senator Glenn. The way the President has presented this and the way it is being talked about around the country, I can tell you from personal experience . . . that the people of this country think this is ready for deployment. They think it is ready to go.

Dr. Cooper. Clearly, we should all work together, then, to disabuse them of that because it is a research program and it is clearly aimed at systems of the distant future.

Senator Glenn. Way distant. Dr. Keyworth, you have followed this thing for a long time. What is your estimate of when this technology may be available to really even consider any of the things we are talking about or even consider it for battlefield use.

Dr. Keyworth. Most certainly, it is some time. Senator Glenn, I agree with virtually every word you have said. You have just described, I think, one of the problems that has precluded much rational discussion of this subject.

If you go back and look at the President's speech . . . you will find that it was entirely research oriented, tentative, searching for new options, and in the future.

The problem, I am afraid, is that the very same desire that drives so many of us to place great emphasis on arms control, has created, let us say, a premature enthusiasm. We are not there yet. We are most certainly nowhere near making a deployment decision.

Senator Glenn. I think there are some things in the President's speech that go well beyond what you have just stated.

I don't have time to go through the speech. I have a copy of the main parts of it here with me, though. He went well beyond what you have just said—calling it just a research program trying to develop this technology.

Dr. Keyworth. I think the accounts of the President's speech did.

Senator Glenn. I have here a *Washington Post* article of March 24 of this year [1984]. The Secretary of Defense is quoted as saying, "What we want to try to get is a system that will develop a defense that is thoroughly reliable and total. I don't see any reason why it can't be done."

Well, I do. It hasn't been invented yet.

Maybe the Secretary of Defense knows something that I am not aware of. I have had every blooming briefing on this subject that I think anybody can possibly have. I think I probably have kept up with the technology of it as closely as any U.S. Senator because of my background and interest in it. It is just not here yet.

The President has misled the people of this country into thinking it is here and now.

Mr. Perle. Senator, the Secretary of Defense is describing an objective. . . . There is no reason to think this is anything other than an objective. Indeed, much of the rhetoric that creates an impression that some deployment is imminent is coming from critics of the program. I picked up the *Washington Post* this morning and read about former Vice President Mondale from [Windom]. I will quote: "President Reagan wants our country to spend hundreds of billions of dollars developing Star Wars missile systems, and at the same time he doesn't want our country to push for the treaty on antisatellite weapons."

This administration has made no decision to spend hundreds of billions of dollars. What we have is a technology development program, a research program. This is clearly spelled out in all of the budget submissions and the testimony is in support of that.

We regret as much as you do the impression that there is imminent deployment because there is not. It is a long-term effort.[14]

Dr. Albert Carnesale, professor of public policy and academic dean at Harvard University's John F. Kennedy School of Government, testified at the same hearing about the vulnerability of a missile defense. He said that defensive technologies evolve as well as the offensive systems to counter them, and that at present the offense had a head start. "Any space-based defense is likely to be more vulnerable than the things it is trying to attack.

"As for thinking about a popup system [one that is launched immediately before use], one must avoid the fallacy of the last move. If we have a popup system that can destroy their missiles in their boost phase, they might have something similar. Suppose they have a popup system, no matter how crude, that is forward-based, say, in their submarines. They know in advance when they are going to launch their offensive missiles and, just before they do so, they pop up a system whose sole function is to shoot down our popup system. It is easier for them than for us, because they control the timing of events. They are not going to be surprised if they are starting a war."[15]

Proponents of the SDI took sharp issue with the critics. At various congressional hearings, SDI advocates charged the skeptics with vastly exaggerating technical problems and generally failing to give the president's plan a fair and unbiased evaluation.

Dr. Robert Jastrow, former director of the Goddard Institute for Space Studies and a leading SDI supporter, told the House Republican Study Committee on August 9, 1984, that scientists opposed to the president's plan had made "serious technical errors" in their assessment of the required weaponry.[16] The critics, he said, hoped to "create a misleading impression that the President's plan is impractical, ineffective, and costly." Jastrow charged, for instance, that both the Union of Concerned Scientists and OTA had vastly overestimated the number of laser satellites that would be needed for a defensive screen against Soviet missiles.

"It is important to note the consequence of the exaggeration," Jastrow said. "Every laser-equipped satellite will cost about as much as a Trident submarine—several billion dollars—and a fleet of thousands of such satellites would cost many trillions of dollars, and would price the President's plan out of reach.

"On the other hand when the correct number of satellites—100 or less—is assumed, the cost drops down to a level which is well within the current annual level of expenditures for U.S. strategic forces."

He also accused SDI critics of overstating the countermeasures that the Soviets could take. "One proposed countermeasure is a protective coating about 1/2" thick, spread over the surface of the Soviet ICBM to protect it from the heat of the laser beam," Jastrow pointed out. "The penalty paid by the Soviets for this countermeasure lies in the fact that for every pound of protective coating there must be some reduction in the weight of the payload carried by the missile; otherwise the missile will fail to achieve its intended range."

Other SDI advocates testified before House hearings that a new assessment of BMDs was justified by a wide range of technological advances and not by a single, major breakthrough.

The Senate Foreign Relations Committee had thoroughly aired questions of costs, technology, and strategic implications associated with High Frontier at a hearing on April 14, 1983. During this session, both Professor George Rathjens of the Massachusetts Institute of Technology and Jan Lodal, former member of the National Security Council, were asked the following questions: Do you believe that technology already exists for deploying a system such as the High Frontier? If not, what breakthroughs do you believe will be necessary before we can deploy such a defense network? Finally, do you believe that the United States can afford to build this type of capability in the absence of vastly increased taxation and without major reductions in other military areas? Their testimony follows:

Dr. Rathjens. I think that is a rather complex question, Senator. One must ask, "Defense of what?" If we are talking about defense of American cities, population and industry, I really think at the present time the situation is fundamentally hopeless. I don't believe that High Frontier or the President's kind of proposals or anything in sight can help very much in providing security for American cities and population.

Forty billion dollars wouldn't scratch the surface. I don't think $200 billion would even begin to make a dent on that kind of problem if we credit the other fellow with any effort at all to overcome what we might do. I don't even think we could defend against his present capabilities, even if he stood still; if he makes a concerted effort to counter what we might do, I am convinced that that problem is hopeless for a very long period of time.

Now, if we are talking about defense of a limited number of Minuteman or MX missile silos, I think that is a very different problem. First of all, we could tolerate the loss of many. They are very difficult targets to destroy as compared with cities. There is some possibility that some kind of a defense of such targets could make sense in a narrow, technical sense.

I do not believe a space-based component would, however, be very helpful. To the extent that defense of hard targets might have attraction at all, the important component would be close-in defense: attempting to destroy the other fellow's warheads when they are almost on the target. But even then, I would have my doubts about whether that would be very attractive.

Mr. Lodal. I think there is an element of truth in both sides of this argument. I think there is a much better chance that General Graham's approach could be deployed for a reasonable cost, whether it is $40 billion or $100 billion, but something less than the trillion dollar numbers that one can easily construct for laser-based systems, and I think it is somewhat harder for the Soviets to come up with simple countermeasures.

But, I believe there would be countermeasures, and as Dr. Rathjens said, that is what makes it so hard to estimate the cost of these things because then you have to go back and redesign and redevelop.

So I think we could afford it and I like his idea of focusing on existing technology, trying to do things in simple ways rather than overly complex ways. Particle beams, for example, I think are completely out of the question and make no sense for us to focus our efforts on. Lasers make a little more sense but not a whole lot more, and his approach of using physical destruction mechanism I think is more sensible.

On the other hand, I think his basic strategic analysis is completely wrong and I think it is internally contradictory. He talks about the terribly unstable situation we arc in today. In fact, we are in a very stable situation. The Soviets don't have anything like a first strike capability because they can't touch our alert bombers; they can't touch our submarines at sea. They in fact can't even do that much against our land-based missiles under some scenarios. And those aren't the way wars start. They start by conventional attack and escalate from there, and those aren't the main problems we have.

His system . . . would bring us closer to a first strike capability, not further away from it.

So I think we could afford it. I think the technology is worth pursuing. I think it is a bad idea from a strategic standpoint, not necessarily a technical standpoint.[17]

General Graham also testified at this hearing on the wide discrepancy in cost estimates for the High Frontier project, ranging from High Frontier's own $15 billion estimate to the Pentagon's $200 to $300 billion price tag. "Now let me tell you how we came up with $15 billion. I think it is interesting. We used technology off the shelf. We used things that people already knew how to manufacture.

We went to the manufacturer and said if we needed 500 of those or 10,000 of those or whatever, how much would it cost? And they told us the cost and we added up all those costs.

"We went to the research and development people and said how much would it cost to put this thing together and test it, and we added that for testing. And we went to space transportation people and said how much would it cost to put these up, either on boosters or by the shuttle, and added that figure in and it comes to $15 billion.

"Now one of the reasons we got rather low unit prices is that in space hardware we have never made but a few things at a time—you know, two or three of these satellites. I think the biggest number we have ever produced so far of a single type was 10. Recently a contract was let for 28 satellites of the same kind. This was an astonishingly big order.

"We are talking about 500 satellites of the same type. We are talking about not building a handful of prototypes but building a lot. And that caused the estimates from industry to drop way down in terms of unit cost because you have practically no R&D tail hanging on to the back end of every item you buy. . . .

"So we stick to our $15 billion. . . .

"If you take 10 or 12 years to do this and use the terribly complex red tape snarled acquisition systems of the Department of Defense, it will indeed cost $50 billion. . . .

"Now the *Air Force Journal* did, in fact, quote $300 billion but as we have told your staff, they were quoting Aerospace Co., which said it would cost $300 billion to do something like High Frontier, but they didn't even have our study in hand, and they came up with a system that involved not 432 satellites, such as we say are necessary, but 9,000 satellites. That is why you got a $300 billion figure, and nobody holds to that $300 billion figure any more in Government."[18]

General Graham also commented on the cost estimate Defense Advanced Research Projects Agency Director Robert Cooper had given to the Senate Armed Services Committee in March 1982. At that time, Dr. Cooper had testified: "Our understanding of systems implications and costs would lead us to project expenditures on the order of $200 to $300 billion in acquisition costs alone for the proposed [High Frontier] system."[19] General Graham observed: "Right. That was in March 1982, Senator Pressler, and at that time High Frontier's idea had hit the Pentagon like a great bomb. They had done very little real work on it. As a matter of fact, I believe it was at that same hearing that Senator Warner asked Dr. Cooper about it and he says High Frontier would be all right but we cannot develop lasers that fast. In other words, he had not read our study and believed we were talking about lasers."

The Defense Department slightly reduced its High Frontier cost assessment after projecting a defense network including about 100 space battle stations, rather than High Frontier's 432. But it remained skeptical about the overall concept. All of this was evident in the testimony of John Gardner, director of defensive systems for the Department of Defense, before the Senate Armed Services Committee on March 23, 1983.

Mr. Gardner. Before we would recommend a significant undertaking on a system like the High Frontier we believe that significantly more work would have to be done in the examination of that system from the viewpoint of its survivability and considering the kinds of responsive threats that might come at that system from the Soviet Union, were they to conclude that it represented a military threat.

So, we believe there would be a considerable amount of work yet to be done before this Nation should undertake a system of that kind. . . .

Senator [Dan] Quayle [(R-Ind.)]. In addition to the technology development issues, what other major uncertainties were identified in the course of this study?

Mr. Gardner. There is a considerable amount of uncertainty relative to the cost of such a system.

Senator Quayle. Is there any way we can get a better handle on the cost because this is going to be something that might be of interest to some of the people up here on the Hill?

Mr. Gardner. Well, we have made estimates of the cost of such a system, using the costing techniques that are common to the Department of Defense for both defensive systems, space launches and satellite systems. It is on the basis of the cost estimates that estimates have been ranging from $50 to $60 billion, and to numbers considerably in excess of that.[20]

A persistent theme running through the testimony on SDI technology was the view that as defensive technologies evolve, so do the offensive systems they must deal with. It was pointed out that the same technology the United States uses to neutralize Soviet missiles can be used by the Soviet Union against U.S. defenses.

Overall, there was general agreement among proponents and opponents of the SDI that the surface of the technological problems involved in any deployment of space defenses had been barely scratched.

11

Strategic Defense Initiative and The European Allies

Although Congress has to date not held hearings on the European reactions to the SDI, the subject is of great concern to many senators and members of the House. The Congressional Research Service of the Library of Congress produced a careful study of the issue in response to questions from Senator William Proxmire (D-Wisc.). Many U.S. legislators have held meetings in the United States or Europe with European leaders. Media reports on European views of the SDI provide additional information. Congressional interest derives from concern that the SDI may adversely affect the NATO alliance, unarguably the most important U.S. military partnership. This chapter summarizes European attitudes on the SDI and some of the potential consequences for the defense of Western Europe.

The president's speech in March 1983 caught European leaders totally by surprise. They have had not only to make up their own minds about what course of action to follow, but also to take into account currents of opinion within their own governments and nations.

Differing views on the SDI welled up within the European bureaucracies. The ministries of defense and foreign affairs within each NATO nation have actively debated the wisdom of the SDI and its impact upon Europe. The French heads of those respective ministries have, for example, actually expressed divergent views about the SDI.[1] Eventually each ministry will probably develop a detailed position on the issue. The prime minister will then attempt to reconcile possible differences between the ministries before the government itself can establish a final policy. This process may take years and involve changes in governing parties.

Each head of government must also come to terms with opinions within his or her own political party. Similarly, the head of government would have to be sure that government policies on the SDI enjoyed majority support within parliament or risk defeat on legislation that might be introduced about the SDI.

Outside of government, European political leaders must consider public opinion as expressed in constituent mail, polls, the media, lobbying efforts by interest groups, and educational efforts by academic institutions or foundations. For example, the British have polled public opinion on the issue of the SDI. The various newspapers in each nation regularly discuss the SDI. Some support the concept as stated by President Reagan; some support part of the idea, such as research; and many resolutely oppose the SDI in any form. Interest groups in Europe, just as in the United States, take an active role in trying to persuade the government and the public regarding the advantages or disadvantages of the SDI. In addition, educational institutes and foundations have organized conferences that have given public officials opportunities to make important public statements on the SDI as well as allow scientists and scholars to be heard.

These sources of opinion and the political and bureaucratic discussions have been the principal features of evolving European views on the SDI since the president's speech of March 23, 1983. Initial reactions by governmental officials were restrained—in part because they were unclear as to the full meaning of the speech. Many also resented not having been consulted prior to its delivery. Those references in the president's address that referred to the present strategic concept as "immoral" troubled most European leaders, who recognize that their nations' defenses depend upon a strategy of nuclear deterrence. Others openly bristled when Secretary Weinberger gave them an "ultimatum" of 60 days to reply to his offer to participate in the research effort.

Conversations between European leaders and a delegation of six U.S. senators (Dole, Thurmond, Laxalt, McClure, Cochran, and Pressler) during the period of April 5–13, 1985, revealed many European questions and doubts regarding the SDI.[2] In England, France, Germany, and Italy, the delegation asked European leaders at the highest level their opinions of the SDI and how they felt it would affect the NATO alliance. The leaders expressed concern that the "Nunn amendment" philosophy would be enhanced by the SDI, particularly if the allies refused to endorse the program. [The Nunn amendment was sponsored by Senator Sam Nunn (D-Ga.) to require our allies to contribute more to NATO or face a reduction in U.S.

contributions. It failed by a margin of 55 to 41 on the Senate floor in June 1984.]

The Europeans also expressed fears that any system that could destroy a weapon in a distant country within seconds after it had been launched could also be used offensively. European defense needs might be ignored should the United States embark on an entirely new national security strategy. However, they gave lukewarm endorsements to SDI research and expressed some interest in having their countries participate in that research. But they were clearly nervous about the potential U.S.–NATO relationship under the SDI. This indicates the importance of the current debate: We are on the cutting edge of a whole new era in the arms race.

Official European knowledge of the SDI derived largely from the president's speech and from briefings given by administration spokespersons, as well as from articles written by journalists. Europeans were curious to know whether the SDI was strictly a Reagan administration phenomenon that might change with a new president, and what role Congress was likely to play in the issue. The Senate delegation explained that Congress was indeed involved and would continue to be vigorously active on the proposal. The European leaders, particularly the Germans, made a plea for closer consultation with the United States and more involvement prior to any definitive U.S. action on the SDI.

From their distant perspective, they observed that the SDI did not seem to be subject to the same careful analysis or policy scrutiny by Congress as other defense projects such as NATO spending or the MX missile.

WEST GERMANY

Helmut Kohl, the chancellor of West Germany and his country's highest elected official, addressed the German Bundestag on April 18, 1985, concerning the SDI. His speech reflected both an interest in the concept and caution about its implications for German national interests.

Although Chancellor Kohl asserted that the strategy of nuclear deterrence was currently indispensable and would remain so for the foreseeable future, he said, "Anyone who seriously desires a far-reaching reduction in the world's nuclear arsenals . . . should carefully ponder all alternative means of safeguarding peace and preventing war."[3] He indicated it was not yet possible to determine whether the SDI would provide that alternative, but insisted, "We should retain the ability to discuss in a serious and far-sighted manner any political visions that can help us to achieve the vital goals of our policies."

Kohl's speech was critical of the minority party Social Democrats' (SPD) resolute opposition to the SDI. The SPD's "global rejection of the SDI before the necessary foundations exist for a decision and before the U.S. Administration has completed its assessment of the research program indicates not only a want of foresight, but also little sense of responsibility," he said. Despite greater hesitation expressed by some of his Free Democrat coalition partners, particularly Foreign Minister Hans Dietrich Genscher, the chancellor said, "In our view, the American research program is therefore justified, politically necessary, and in the interest of overall Western security. My government therefore basically supports the American research project on strategic defense."

Referring to his February 9, 1985, statement on the SDI to the Military Science Symposium in Munich, Chancellor Kohl repeated certain conditions that would govern West Germany's evolving consideration of the SDI:

- Europe's security must not be decoupled from that of the United States.
- NATO's strategy of flexible response must remain fully valid as long as no more promising alternative is found for preventing war.
- Instability must be avoided during any transition from a purely deterrent strategy to a new form of strategic stability that is more reliant on defensive systems.
- Disparities must be eliminated, and the emergence of new threats below the nuclear level avoided.

The chancellor also stressed the special importance of the arms control dimension of the SDI issue: "In the Federal Government's view it is essential that before any decisions are taken that go beyond research, cooperative solutions should be sought which will ensure that strategic stability will be maintained and where possible improved, nuclear offensive potentials will be drastically reduced, and the relationship between offensive and defensive systems will be jointly defined to guarantee the largest degree of stability at the lowest possible level of armaments."

He specified that German participation in SDI research should guarantee fair partnership and a free exchange of findings, should "not remain a technological one-way street," and should secure for Germany "a self-contained sphere of research" and permit it to exercise influence on the overall project.

Chancellor Kohl's cautious support for the research aspect of the SDI stands in contrast to the views of his domestic political opponents as well as some members of his own party. Opposition SPD leaders have argued that the research effort alone would accelerate the arms race because both the Soviet Union and the United States would further develop the offensive capabilities needed to overcome a defensive shield. Horst Ehmke of the SPD argued that the program would force the Europeans to "become an appendix of the United States military industrial complex." Defense Minister Manfred Woerner pessimistically warned in a 1984 television interview that Western European defense could become decoupled from the United States and pointed out that the SDI seemed to be designed only for protection against ICBMs aimed at the United States.

The antiestablishment Green party prepared to make the SDI a campaign issue in their effort to secure more seats in West Germany's 1985 state elections.

GREAT BRITAIN

Official British reaction to the idea of the SDI was slightly warmer than that of other nations. Prime Minister Margaret Thatcher, following a meeting with President Reagan at Camp David on December 22, 1984, expressed official interest in the potential for the SDI, but cautioned that negotiations would have to precede deployment.[4] She set forth four points of agreement:

- The U.S. and Western aim is not to achieve superiority but to maintain balance.
- SDI-related deployment would have to be a matter for negotiation because of treaty requirements.
- The overall aim is to enhance, not undercut, deterrence.
- East/West negotiations should aim to achieve security with reduced levels of offensive systems on both sides.[5]

Mrs. Thatcher has also indicated on several occasions that Britain has an interest in participating in the SDI research program. During 1985, however, there were signs of more restraint in British official views of the SDI and a definite decision to participate in the European EUREKA technology development program.

One reason for reservations about the SDI centers on the program's potential to undermine Britain's own nuclear deterrence—particularly the modernization of its Trident submarine fleet. A lucid explanation of the situation was written by Dr. Farooq Hussain, director of studies at the Royal United Services Institute for Defense Studies in London: "When Britain and France planned the modernisation of their strategic nuclear forces they had to make long-term assumptions about the Soviet Union's ability to defend itself against missiles. The independent credibility of the nuclear forces of medium powers depends on what has become known in strategic jargon as a 'de-capitation strike'. Such a strike should threaten Moscow and, if possible, all other centres of military and political command and control. When the British government came to decide on a replacement for its aging fleet of Polaris submarines, one of the attractions of the Trident system was that it would significantly increase the number of warheads available. Although Britain's planners had considered in detail the likely developments in anti-ballistic missile technologies, they could not have anticipated the prospect of the Strategic Defense Initiative. Although everyone accepts that even a near leak-proof ballistic missile defence will not come to pass within the lifetime of the British Trident fleet, very significant improvements in anti-missile capabilities are feasible within the next 10 to 15 years.

"Thus, if there are no constraints on the development of space-based weapons, the effectiveness of Britain's nuclear fleet as an independent deterrent will be seriously jeopardised just at the time when Britain is bearing the heaviest burden of the cost of the Trident programme. Not only will the new technology for intercepting ballistic missile re-entry vehicles undermine the independent credibility of the forces, but the development of anti-satellite weapons will put at risk the ability of the British and the French governments to command and control their fleets."[6]

A significant shift in the official British attitude toward the SDI occurred on March 15, 1985, when British Foreign Secretary Sir Geoffrey Howe delivered an address calling attention to some reservations about the program. It was never absolutely clear whether Prime Minister Thatcher had approved the speech in advance, but it is highly unlikely that she did not approve at least in principle the essence of the remarks. After commenting rather briefly on the importance of President Reagan's initiative, particularly in response to the attention it focused on the considerable Soviet research underway in BMD and ASAT activities, Howe spent the remainder of his lengthy speech expressing doubts about the SDI. "There would inevitably be risks in a radical alteration of the present basis for western security. How far would these risks be offset by the attractions of adopting a more defensive posture: this is to say, of developing what might prove to be only a limited defence against weapons of devastating destructive force? Could the process of moving towards a greater emphasis on active defences be managed without generating dangerous uncertainty?

". . . Would the establishment of limited defences increase the threat to civilian populations by stimulating a return to the targeting policies of the 1950s?

"Most fundamental of all, would the supposed technology actually work? And would it . . . provide defences that not only worked but were survivable and cost-effective?

". . . There would be no advantage in creating a new Maginot Line of the twenty-first century, liable to be outflanked by relatively simpler and demonstrably cheaper counter-measures.

"What are the chances that there would be no outright winner in the everlasting marathon of the arms race? . . . How would protection be extended against the non-ballistic nuclear threat, the threat posed by aircraft or cruise missiles, battlefield nuclear weapons or, in the last resort, by covert action?"

Sir Geoffrey raised other concerns: Were there not better systems to protect military installations? Was the cost not disproportionate to the value? Would not new defensive systems lead to increased levels of offensive nuclear systems? After posing several other questions, he stressed that "there are no easy answers, that the risks may outweigh the benefits, that science may not be able to provide a safer solution to the nuclear dilemma of the past forty years than we have found already—all these points underline the importance of proceeding with the utmost deliberation."[7]

The tone of the speech was undeniably skeptical of the SDI. U.S. Assistant Secretary of Defense Richard Perle reacted sharply. He referred to Howe's manner of questioning the SDI as "tendentious" and his account of Soviet–U.S. relations as "unrecognizable to anyone who has charted [their] course."[8]

British public opinion is also divided on the SDI issue. An early 1985 Gallup poll found a fairly even division among a random sampling of the population on various aspects of the SDI program.[9] The (London) *Times* and the *Daily Telegram* are supportive of the SDI, whereas many other publications are opposed. The British Labor party is resolutely opposed, and many members of the Conservative party are skeptical.

In late May, the British government decided to accept the invitation of France to participate in the EUREKA research effort, although retaining its option of also participating in the U.S. program. This may signal no more than a desire to accommodate its European partners. It may point the way toward weakening British support for participation in SDI research, or even of support for the SDI concept itself. Official British support for participation in SDI research seemed assured when, on December 6, 1985, the U.S. and British defense secretaries signed a memorandum of understanding specifying 18 SDI-related research areas in which British involvement would be sought.

FRANCE

Of all the allies, the French were the most openly critical of the SDI concept. The first major official criticism of the idea was expressed on June 12, 1984, when the French representative to the Committee on Disarmament in Geneva called upon both the United States and the Soviet Union to cease efforts to improve BMD systems. He stated that "the announcement alone of the intention to go forward with the refining of such systems constitutes in itself a spur to redouble the effort to build offensive systems: each [of the two] powers will seek to saturate the envisaged antiballistic systems of the other party and to multiply non-ballistic systems."[10] He reiterated earlier French calls for negotiations to limit the development of high-orbit ASAT weapons and for a five-year moratorium on the testing or deployment of "guided-energy weapons systems."

Subsequent to this remark, other French officials began to take slightly harder lines. In August, Foreign Minister Claude Cheysson used the discomfiting analogy of the SDI being a Maginot line in space. The reference was to the massive line of defensive fortifications constructed by France after World War I to prevent a German invasion, but which the Germans easily circumvented in 1940. He posed a rhetorical question: "Remember the Maginot line during the late thirties. The countries it did not protect . . . lost confidence in the alliance which bound them to us: could these European countries, which are allies of the United States—a United States which would feel protected by a network of killer missiles—still have faith in U.S. protection?"[11]

In December 1984, President François Mitterand publicly described the SDI as a program for "overarmament." "One should be moving towards disarmament," he said, "that is, towards balance at the lowest possible level." He renewed the call for negotiations on space.

More severe comments came in February 1985 from Minister of Defense Charles Henru during a Wehrkunde (defense studies) conference in Munich. Henru asserted that the development of a successful missile defense could lead the two superpowers into a "complicity" that "would rid them of any rivalry" in the strategic arena. That, however, would leave Europe in a less stable situation than it now enjoyed. In particular, France's own nuclear deterrence would be undercut.[12]

The specter of a useless French nuclear force received widespread attention when the distinguished French actor Yves Montand narrated in April 1985 a controversial television program depicting the Soviet invasion of France. Montand's main assertion was that France had failed to keep pace with military strategy and was relying too heavily upon nuclear deterrence. Instead the emphasis should be on conventional warfare, including chemical weapons. Montand also warned that Reagan's Star Wars initiative might leave Western Europe at the mercy of the two superpowers—"Europe would be totally disarmed, naked. . . . If both the two superpowers managed to construct such a defensive system, then our deterrent wouldn't have much since . . . all, or almost all, our missiles would be intercepted and diverted."[13] Other observers pointed to favorable comments made by Montand about the imaginativeness and relatively low cost of the SDI.[14]

It was also during April that France initiated its own high-technology research program, EUREKA. The most striking manifestation of French opposition to U.S. goals in the SDI occurred during a May summit meeting in Bonn, when President Mitterand rejected the U.S. offer to participate in the SDI research effort. Subsequently, France has blocked efforts on the part of the United States to gain a statement of support from the NATO allies.

There are supporters of the SDI in France,[15] but it is the government that charts the nation's defense policy course. Mitterand has indicated his intention to remain in office as president even if his Socialist party should lose control of the National Assembly. For the time being, France seems to hold the trump card in the game of SDI diplomacy in Europe.

ITALY

Speaking to a joint session of the U.S. Congress, Italian Prime Minister Bettino Craxi stated on March 6, 1985 that Italians "view with interest the research program for the strategic defense initiative announced by President Reagan. Such a program appears to us as completely compatible with the existence of the ABM treaty . . . ." Over 60 Italian SDI research proposals have since been offered for U.S. consideration, and Italian and U.S. officials continue to consult on a formal agreement for possible Italian participation in the SDI.

INDEPENDENT SDI RESEARCH BY EUROPEAN NATIONS: EUREKA

The European allies of the United States are giving increasingly serious consideration to the development of a research effort independent of the U.S. SDI program. One motive for such an undertaking stems from a general desire to keep abreast of U.S. and Japanese technology. Technological research that has commercial as well as military applications could help to stem European perceptions that they have fallen behind in the struggle for technological competitiveness. Some Europeans believe Europe should not be totally subordinate to U.S. leadership in respect to space and high-technology research, as might be the case if they simply accepted without reservation the U.S. invitation to participate in the SDI research program. A separate European research undertaking would allow them not only to keep a comfortable distance from aspects of the SDI that they dislike or question but also to support in general terms U.S. research on the SDI.

One of the first to articulate the necessity of a common European approach to the SDI was Jacques Delors of France, president of the European Commission, which is the Common Market's executive body. In late March 1985, Delors exhorted the ten-member group to take a "common stand" on SDI research, and warned that "if the Europeans act separately, they will diminish their chance of negotiating participation." On March 29, he proposed to the summit meeting of the Common Market leaders a doubling of the percentage of the European Economic Community budget for research and technology—from 3 to 6 percent.[16]

Further highly important steps were taken toward European space and high-technology research in Paris in mid-April. The French cabinet discussed a specific French proposal for such an effort—the European Research Coordination Agency, nicknamed EUREKA. Specific areas of potential cooperation included high-powered computers, lasers, artificial intelligence, and micro-processors. The French Foreign Ministry formally conveyed the offer to other European governments the following week. In explaining the proposal during a television interview, the French minister of defense emphasized that EUREKA would promote "peace in the stars." He stated that countries other than the United States and Soviet Union should be allowed to acquire space-age technologies such as military observation satellites. The United States, he continued, should not be allowed "to place us in a kind of economic super-NATO . . . on the pretext of chasing after our industries, our techniques, our knowledge, our technologies and our brains."[17]

On April 23, 1985, a meeting of the recently revived Western European Union failed to agree on a joint response to the SDI invitation from the United States. French Foreign Minister Roland Dumas warned that if Europeans failed to define "our own needs, our own interests and our own objectives," participation in the U.S. program would bring few benefits to Europe. He stated that the absence of a European position would give the United States a "blank check for undertakings that even those responsible for them say are uncertain, that could be damaging to our immediate security. Rather than responding in disorder, or negatives, to the American offer what is necessary is a mobilization of the Europeans that will enable this cooperation to be something other than resignation."[18] Only Italy and Luxembourg, however, endorsed the French EUREKA proposal. Great Britain and, to a lesser extent, West Germany were unprepared to issue a joint communiqué.[19]

The stage was set for the most dramatic act to date in the struggle for an independent European research program. French President François Mitterand announced on May 4, 1985, at the Bonn summit meeting that France would not participate in the U.S. research program "in its present form." He cited as one of the reasons a reference made by President Reagan to the European role as that of "subcontractors." Mitterand reportedly informed President Reagan of his decision during a private meeting two days earlier. The news was both unwelcome and unexpected, as the United States sought to avoid a formal mention of the SDI at the summit meeting to avoid the appearance of divisiveness among the allies.[20]

Subsequent to the summit meeting, the EUREKA project has gained support. During the week of May 20, the West German and British foreign ministers paid official visits to Paris where they voiced support for the French idea. West German Foreign Minister Hans Dietrich Genscher called for a "coordinated" European response to the SDI. "Europe," he said, "must not drop to the level of subcontractor and supplier. It must unite its technological capabilities so that it can be an equal partner of the United States." British Foreign Secretary Sir Geoffrey Howe expressed a similar willingness to participate in EUREKA during private conversations with the French foreign minister.[21] Both the British and West Germans, however, stressed that they did not see participation in EUREKA as incompatible with participation in the

U.S. effort. On May 28, 1985, West Germany announced it had agreed with France to establish a European research program for space and advanced technologies.[22] On June 2, a British spokesperson announced that the foreign secretary had notified his French counterpart that Britain would participate in the EUREKA program.[23]

The NATO Council, consisting of the foreign ministers of the 16 NATO nations, issued a final joint communiqué on June 7, 1985, expressing support for the U.S. arms control-negotiating effort with the Soviet Union in Geneva. However, French opposition and the hesitation of other council members resulted in no mention of the SDI in the communiqué. This was seen by some observers as a rebuff to the United States, which had worked to obtain the council's endorsement for the SDI.[24]

The communiqué said, "We strongly support U.S. efforts in all three areas of negotiation, and we call on the Soviet Union to adopt a positive approach." The three areas included "preventing an arms race in space and terminating it on earth, . . . limiting and reducing nuclear arms, and . . . strengthening strategic capability."

U.S. Secretary of State George Shultz, British Foreign Minister Howe, and NATO Secretary-General Lord Carrington indicated in separate news conferences that the NATO ministers agreed on the necessity for U.S. SDI research as a counter to Soviet space weapons research.

Thus, it is clear that the United States' most important military and economic partners had given thoughtful consideration to the U.S. request for their participation in SDI research. A concerted effort was made in 1984 and 1985 to develop a joint European response to the request, a response that avoided offending the United States or undercutting its arms control-negotiating position and NATO unity. European officials publicly discussed their concerns about the implications much as the members of the U.S. Congress did, and their conclusions as of June 1985 were also similar. That is, they were not prepared to unequivocally reject or endorse the SDI, realizing that the program was a research effort that for years would try to unravel scientific, mathematical, and engineering uncertainties. By the end of 1985 the British government had worked out an agreement with the United States for the collaboration of British scientists and companies in SDI research. U.S. officials were confident that additional agreements with other allied governments would follow.

12

The Role of Congress in Assessing
A New Strategic Program

The SDI debates in Congress provide a classic example of how Congress struggles to properly assess and initiate a complex new strategic proposal. Indeed, the SDI debate is even more complicated in that its ultimate result is still a concept. Congress finds itself starting a massive new program of which no one knows for certain the possible results.

President Reagan's decision in March 1983 to intensify research on antimissile technology presented Congress and the U.S. people, as well as the governmental and nongovernmental research community, with a bold challenge. That challenge has been met only partially. It will continue to confront the U.S. public and their elected officials in Washington. It is clear that the congressional and public debate on the SDI has raised questions and offered tentative answers that will recur in the debates of the next several years.

In other words, the essential framework for analysis of the SDI concept is already in place, having been developed in large measure by the debate in Congress and by the testimony of the executive branch and of public proponents and critics of the initiative. During this process, Congress considered and voted on many alternative proposals—to reduce or increase funding for the SDI and ASAT programs and to micromanage various aspects of that funding.

As is the case with most major policy decisions in the national government, the president and the executive branch have taken, and will continue to hold, the initiative on this important national security program. The role of Congress, while limited to a more reactive part in the definition of defense policy, is not insignificant or inconclusive. Congress is the keeper of the national purse, and it takes seriously its "doubting Thomas" role whenever the stakes are high, as they are with the SDI. The congressional debate on the SDI leads to several observations concerning Congress in action on complex strategic issues:

1. When there is doubt about the wisdom of pursuing a particular course recommended by the executive branch, Congress goes through an anguishingly complex process before making a decision.

2. Concerning defense policymaking, Congress often is persuaded by convincing arguments based on perceptions of Soviet misbehavior.

3. Congress finds it easier to support major spending for research in defense technologies than actual procurement and deployment of new weapons systems.

4. Congress is sensitive to U.S. treaty obligations and to the arms control process, and is especially conscious of the need to avoid complicating the already difficult task of U.S. arms control negotiators.

5. On a complex national security issue such as the SDI, Congress usually opts for the "conservative hard-line" position. That is, when there is much uncertainty about a presidential defense initiative, Congress will critically debate, but almost inevitably err on the side of spending more rather than less. This is especially true if the defense initiative is defined as "research."

6. Congressional testimony on controversial subjects such as ASATs and the SDI tends to be repetitive. For example, several committees in both houses have held hearings on space weapons, and a relatively small number of witnesses have appeared over and over again at those hearings.

7. Defense and foreign policy issues often are not clearly distinguishable, with the respective defense and international affairs committees sharing and sometimes competing in the development of congressional policy. This rivalry of the international affairs committees and the defense committees helps develop a more thorough legislative record and understanding. However, it can also lead to a divisiveness which has not yet occurred with the SDI.

8. Congress seeks out and defers to expertise on highly technical issues, including both the executive branch and private groups and individuals. Congress has confidence in the ability of defense scientists to tackle and solve technical or scientific problems.

9. On the whole, Congress supports technological solutions to military problems, but it is reluctant to endorse a comprehensive "push-button" defense strategy that could minimize the role of human deliberation prior to specific military action.

10. Congress is cost conscious about defense spending, but if it becomes convinced of the merits of a new technology it is prepared to spend enormous amounts. The SDI and ASAT research programs—which together will be more expensive than any other weapons research program in history—indicate the lengths to which Congress will go to seek security for the people of the United States.

11. It is clear that Congress has avoided simplistic arguments and has identified many of the principal strategic issues surrounding the SDI, as

well as some of the technological issues. At this point, most members of Congress realize that we simply do not know enough to make a conclusive judgment on a new strategic doctrine. Congress has approached this question in an incremental fashion and has approved the first step by providing funding for research. This does not necessarily mean Congress will continue to increase SDI research funding, let alone approve advanced testing that could phase into prototype development and testing. However, if the SDI follows the pattern of most recent major weapons systems, it will be approved on a geometrically expanding basis.

Congress will continue to ask probing questions, and reports of successes or failures in the research already underway will be seized upon by partisans on either side of the SDI concept as evidence supporting their case. But such reports will seem inconclusive to most members of Congress, at least until more comprehensive analysis and testimony are provided through additional hearings and briefings. Furthermore, the research is so entrenched that testing seems likely to occur.

The House and Senate face many more decisions on ASATs and the SDI, and will expect to see or hear answers to the following questions before giving the green light to full-scale development, testing, and procurement: Will the SDI contribute to nuclear weapons reductions, or increased nuclear instability? Could computer errors aboard a space-based anti-ICBM compound the ever-present possibility of war by accident? Are there risks in unilateral or bilateral deployment of SDI systems? What are the potential effects on the NATO alliance and other U.S. mutual defense commitments?

In addition to these specific questions, Congress has not yet resolved the following very fundamental issues on the SDI. These basic issues will form the crux of the continuing congressional SDI debate:

1. The capacity of advanced technology to make nuclear weapons less threatening, if not obsolete.
2. The identification of specific advanced development and deployment objectives for antimissile systems.
3. The potential cost of such systems, particularly in the context of the estimated cost of potential countermeasures that could be anticipated from an adversary.
4. The arms control treaty restrictions on advanced development, testing, and deployment of antimissile systems, primarily those arising under the ABM treaty.
5. The effect of BMDs on the likelihood of nuclear war.

These questions will not be answered definitively in the near future, and some would argue that it is premature to expect immediate answers. However, unlike the decision to implement the strategy of deterrence, the decision to move forward to a strategy of enhanced deterrence based on the SDI will be considered in depth over a considerable length of time, perhaps decades. This affords the U.S. people and their elected officials the expensive luxury of thorough consideration of all the possible ramifications of this decision. In this instance, the technology does not exist in perfected form, and the strategy can and will be exhaustively debated before we know whether the technology can be developed to support it.

Humanity's dream of a perfect defense may not be realized, but the search for that invincibility will continue to occupy our best minds, our greatest efforts, and many of our resources. The Congress must continue to devote a major amount of its time to resolving what probably will be the most expensive and extensive strategic program in all human history.

Notes

PREFACE

1. *Cong. Rec.*, June 4, 1985, 99th Cong., 1st Sess., 131 (72): S7353.
2. Ibid., S7340.
3. Ibid., June 5, 1985 131 (73): S7375–77.
4. Ibid., June 4, 1985, 131 (72): S7340.

CHAPTER 1

1. "Address before the General Assembly of the United Nations on Peaceful Uses of Atomic Energy," December 8, 1953. Dwight D. Eisenhower in *Public Papers of the Presidents of the United States,* Washington: GPO, 1953, 813–22.
2. *Washington Post,* October 16, 1983, B4.
3. "Statement on Deployment of the Anti-Ballistic Missile System," March 14, 1969. Richard Nixon in *Public Papers of the Presidents,* 1969, 216.
4. House Committee on Armed Services, *Defense Department Authorization and Oversight,* H.A.S.C. 98–6, 98th Cong., 1st Sess., March–April 1983, 1370.

CHAPTER 2

1. U.S. Library of Congress. Congressional Research Service. *"Star Wars": Antisatellites and Space-Based BMD.* Issue Brief No. IB81123, by Marcia S. Smith, February 20, 1985 (continually updated). Washington, 1985, 2–7, 12.
2. U.S. Library of Congress. Congressional Research Service. *Space Shuttle.* Issue Brief No. IB81175, by Marcia S. Smith, February 19, 1985 (continually updated). Washington, 1985, 8–9.
3. *Cong. Rec.*, May 6, 1981, 97th Cong., 1st Sess., 127 (68): S4449–50.
4. Ibid., February 2, 1983, 98th Cong., 1st Sess., 129 (8): S926–27.
5. Ibid., February 3, 1983, 129 (9): S1082.
6. Senate Committee on Foreign Relations, *Nomination of Kenneth L. Adelman,* S. Hrg. 98–2, 98th Cong., 1st Sess., January 27 and February 3, 16, and 24, 1983, 104–6.
7. Senate Committee on Foreign Relations, *Controlling Space Weapons,* S. Hrg. 98–141, 98th Cong., 1st Sess., April 14 and May 18, 1983, 112–14.
8. *Cong. Rec.*, July 14, 1983, 98th Cong., 1st Sess., 129 (98): S10027.
9. Ibid., S10028.
10. Ibid., July 18, 1983, 129 (101): S10261.
11. Ibid., S10261–62.
12. Ibid., May 23, 1984, 98th Cong., 2nd Sess., 130 (69): S6366–67.
13. Ibid., S6368.

CHAPTER 3

1. Senate Committee on Foreign Relations, *Controlling Space Weapons,* S. Hrg. 98–141, 98th Cong., 1st Sess., April 14 and May 18, 1983, 11.

2. Senate Committee on Foreign Relations, Subcommittee on Arms Control, Oceans, International Operations, and Environment, *Arms Control and the Militarization of Space,* Hearing on S. Res. 129, 97th Cong., 2d Sess., September 20, 1982, 54–55 (hereinafter cited as *Militarization of Space*).

3. Senate Committee on Foreign Relations, *The SALT II Treaty,* Part 1, 96th Cong., 2d Sess., July 10, 1979, 289.

4. *Militarization of Space,* 10.

5. Senate Committee on Foreign Relations, *Strategic Defense and Anti-Satellite Weapons,* S. Hrg. 98–750, 98th Cong., 2d Sess., April 25, 1984, 62–64 (hereinafter cited as *Anti-Satellite Weapons*).

6. Senate Committee on Armed Services, *Department of Defense Authorization for Appropriations for Fiscal Year 1985,* S. Hrg. 98–724, Part 7, 98th Cong., 2d Sess., April 12, 1984, 3526 (hereinafter cited as *FY1985 Defense Authorization*).

7. Ibid., 3537.

8. *Cong. Rec.,* January 26, 1984, 98th Cong., 2d Sess., 130 (89): S213.

9. *FY1985 Defense Authorization,* 3537.

10. House Committee on Appropriations, Subcommittee on the Department of Defense, *Department of Defense Appropriations for 1985,* Part 2, 98th Cong., 2d Sess., March 6, 1984, 190.

11. Ibid., 191.

12. *Anti-Satellite Weapons,* 12, 56.

13. Senate Committee on Foreign Relations, *Outer Space Arms Control Negotiations,* S. Rpt. 98–342, 98th Cong., 1st Sess., November 18, 1983, 11, 14–15 (hereinafter cited as *Outer Space Arms Control Negotiations*).

14. Letter from President Ronald Reagan to George Bush, President of the U.S. Senate, March 31, 1984.

15. Office of Technology Assessment, *Arms Control in Space: Workshop Proceedings,* Washington: GPO, May 1984, 43.

16. Ibid., 2.

17. R. Jeffrey Smith, "Aerospace Experts Challenge ASAT Decision," *Science* 224 (May 18, 1984): 693–96.

18. *Anti-Satellite Weapons,* 78.

19. Senate Committee on Foreign Relations, *Arms Control Overview,* S. Hrg. 98–939, 98th Cong., 2d Sess., June 13, 1984, 36.

20. House Committee on Foreign Affairs, *The Role of Arms Control in U.S. Defense Policy,* 98th Cong., 2d Sess., June 21, 1984, 105–6.

21. White House, *Report to the Congress on U.S. Policy on ASAT Arms Control,* March 31, 1984, 7.

22. *Outer Space Arms Control Negotiations,* 8–9.

CHAPTER 4

1. *Cong. Rec.,* May 26, 1983, 98th Cong., 1st Sess., 129 (74): H3400–11, and June 14, 1983, 129 (84): H3901–11.

2. House Committee on Armed Services, Subcommittee on Research and Development and Subcommittee on Investigations, *H.R. 3073, People Protection Act,* H.A.S.C. 98-21, 98th Cong., 1st Sess., November 10, 1983.

3. *Cong. Rec.,* May 23, 1984, 98th Cong., 2d Sess., 130 (69): H4405. Additional quotations in this chapter are from ibid., H4406–9 and H4716–38.

CHAPTER 5

1. Quotations and information from this debate are found in *Cong. Rec.*, June 12, 1984, 98th Cong., 2d Sess., 130 (79): S6930–74.
2. Helen Dewar, "Anti-Satellite Tests Backed, with Condition," *Washington Post*, June 13, 1984, A9.

CHAPTER 6

1. President Reagan's Speech on Defense Spending and Defensive Technology, in *Weekly Compilation of Presidential Documents* 19 (12): 423–66.
2. Senate Committee on Armed Services, *Department of Defense Authorization for Appropriations for Fiscal Year 1984*, S. Hrg. 98–49, Part 5, 98th Cong., 1st Sess., March 23, 1983, 2651–54.
3. House Committee on Appropriations, Subcommittee on Defense, *Department of Defense Appropriations for 1984*, Part 8, 98th Cong., 1st Sess., March 23, 1983, 452.
4. *New York Times*, March 4, 1985, Al.

CHAPTER 7

1. House comments on the president's SDI speech are from *Cong. Rec.*, March 24, 1983, 98th Cong., 1st Sess., 129 (39): H1700–2.
2. Ibid., April 7, 1983, 129 (42): H1853–54.
3. House Committee on Armed Services, Subcommittee on Research and Development and Subcommittee on Investigations, *H.R. 3073, People Protection Act*, H.A.S.C. 98–21, 98th Cong., 1st Sess., November 10, 1983, 3.
4. Ibid., 4.
5. Ibid., 5.
6. Ibid., 106.
7. Ibid., 42.
8. House Committee on Armed Services, *Defense Department Authorization and Oversight*, H.A.S.C. 98–34, Part 4, 98th Cong., 2d Sess., March 1, 1984, 475–514; House Committee on Appropriations, Subcommittee on Defense Appropriations, *Department of Defense Appropriations for 1985*, Part 5, 98th Cong., 2d Sess., May 9, 1984, 665–829, 830–955, 1048–51; Senate Committee on Armed Services, *Department of Defense Authorization for Appropriations for Fiscal Year 1985*, S. Hrg. 98–724, Part 6, March 8 and 22 and April 24, 1984, and Part 7, March 15, 1984, 3437–81; Senate Committee on Appropriations, Subcommittee on Defense Appropriations, *Department of Defense Appropriations, FY 85*. S. Hrg. 98–361, Part 3, 98th Cong., 2d Sess., May 15, 1984, 289–439.
9. House Committee on Foreign Affairs, *The Role of Arms Control in U.S. Defense Policy*, 98th Cong., 2d Sess., June 21 and 26 and July 25, 1984.
10. Senate Committee on Foreign Relations, *Strategic Defense and Anti-Satellite Weapons*, S. Hrg. 98–750, 98th Cong., 2d Sess., April 25, 1984; Senate Committee on Foreign Relations, *East–West Cooperation in Outer Space*, S Hrg. 98–1064, 98th Cong., 2d Sess., September 13, 1984.
11. *Cong. Rec.*, May 23, 1984, 98th Cong., 2d Sess., 130 (69): H4405–9.

12. Ibid., May 24, 1984, 130 (70): H4776.

13. Ibid., June 13, 1984, 130 (80): S7120–21.

14. Ibid., S7122–23.

15. Ibid., S7135–39.

16. Ibid., June 19, 1984, 130 (84): S7627–28.

17. Ibid., October 3, 1984, 130 (129): S13198.

18. Senate Committee on Armed Services, *National Defense Authorization Act for Fiscal Year 1986*, S. Rpt. 99–41, 99th Cong., 1st Sess., April 29, 1985, 165–67.

19. *Cong. Rec.*, May 17, 1985, 99th Cong., 1st Sess., 131 (65): S6415–85.

20. All quotations and information on the ASAT amendments are from ibid., May 24, 1985, 131 (70): S7157–75.

21. All information from the June 3, 1985, debate is from ibid., June 3, 1985, 131 (71): S7275–91.

22. All information from the June 4, 1985, debate is from ibid., June 4, 1985, 131 (72): S7325–72.

23. Ibid., June 5, 1985, 131 (73): S7474–78.

24. Ibid., May 15, 1985, 131 (63): H3214.

25. This and the following extracts appear in ibid., June 20, 1985, 131 (83): H4553–636.

26. Ibid., June 26, 1985, 131 (88): H4959–77.

27. Ibid., June 24, 1985, 131 (85): E2964–65.

28. U.S. Department of Defense, *Soviet Military Power 1985*, 4th ed., Washington: GPO, April 1985.

29. *Cong. Rec.*, June 26, 1985, 99th Cong., 1st Sess., 131 (88; Part II): H5015–16, H5019, H5025–26.

CHAPTER 8

1. Synopses of these and other treaties are provided in U.S. Department of State, *Treaties in Force: A List of Treaties and Other International Agreements of the United States in Force on January 1, 1985*, Pub. No. 9433, Washington: GPO, 1985. More detailed information is available in U.S. Arms Control and Disarmament Agency, *Arms Control and Disarmament Agreements: Texts and Histories of Negotiations*, Washington: GPO, 1982.

2. Cited in Senate Committee on Foreign Relations, *United States–Soviet Relations*, S. Hrg. 98–174, Part 2, 98th Cong., 1st Sess., June 22, 1983, 175 (hereinafter cited as *United States–Soviet Relations*).

3. Senate Committee on Armed Services, *Department of Defense Authorization for Appropriations for Fiscal Year 1985*, S. Hrg. 98–724, Part 6, 98th Cong., 2d Sess., March 8, 1984, 2918.

4. Senate Committee on Foreign Relations, *Controlling Space Weapons*, S. Hrg. 98–141, 98th Cong., 1st Sess., April 14, 1983, 27 (hereinafter cited as *Controlling Space Weapons*).

5. *United States–Soviet Relations*, 171–82.

6. House Committee on Foreign Affairs, Subcommittee on International Security and Scientific Affairs, *Arms Control in Outer Space*, 98th Cong., 2d Sess., May 2, 1984, 117.

7. Senate Committee on Armed Services, *Department of Defense Authorization for Appropriations for Fiscal Year 1984*, S. Hrg. 98–49, Part 5, 98th Cong., 1st Sess., May 2, 1983, 2861–62.

8. Senate Committee on Foreign Relations, *Strategic Defense and Anti-Satellite Weapons*, S. Hrg. 98–750, 98th Cong., 2d Sess., April 25, 1984, 213.

9. *Controlling Space Weapons*, 53.

10. Ibid.

11. Senate Committee on Foreign Relations, *Outer Space Arms Control Negotiations*, S. Rpt. 98–342, 98th Cong., 1st Sess., November 18, 1983, 14.

12. Letter from Brent Scowcroft to President Ronald Reagan, March 21, 1984.

13. Office of Technology Assessment, *Arms Control in Space: Workshop Proceedings*, Washington: GPO, May 1984, 33–34.

14. U.S. Department of Defense, *Report to the Congress on the Strategic Defense Initiative*, April 1985, B–1, B–2.

15. Ibid., B–3.

CHAPTER 9

1. This and following quotations from Senator Wallop are taken from Senate Committee on Armed Services, *Department of Defense Authorization for Appropriations for Fiscal Year 1984*, S. Hrg. 98–49, Part 5, 98th Cong., 1st Sess., May 2, 1983, 2858–63.

2. Ibid., 2867–68.

3. Ibid., 2868–69.

4. Senate Committee on Armed Services, *Department of Defense Authorization for Appropriations for Fiscal Year 1985*, S. Hrg. 98–724, Part 6, 98th Cong., 2d Sess., March 8, 1984, 2924–27.

5. Senate Committee on Foreign Relations, *Strategic Defense and Anti-Satellite Weapons*, S. Hrg. 98–750, 98th Cong., 2d Sess., April 25, 1984, 135–136 (hereinafter cited as *Anti-Satellite Weapons*). The full text of the Hoffman Report, *Ballistic Missile Defenses and U.S. National Security*, appears in ibid., 125–40.

6. House Republican Study Committee, *The Strategic Defense Initiative: Deterring War and Defending Mankind*, 98th Cong., 2d Sess., August 9, 1984, 11 (hereinafter cited as Republican Study Committee Hearing).

7. House Committee on Armed Services, Subcommittee on Research and Development and Subcommittee on Investigations, *H.R. 3073, People Protection Act*, H.A.S.C. 98–21, 98th Cong., 1st Sess., November 10, 1983, 101.

8. Republican Study Committee Hearing, 48.

9. House Committee on Foreign Affairs, Subcommittee on International Security and Scientific Affairs, *Arms Control in Outer Space*, 98th Cong., 2d Sess., May 2, 1984, 133–35.

10. *Anti-Satellite Weapons*, 213–15.

11. Republican Study Committee Hearing, 38–39.

12. *Anti-Satellite Weapons*, 85–86.

13. Ibid., 87.

14. Ibid., 180.

15. Ibid., 59.

16. Ibid., 59–60.

17. Ibid., 69.

18. Ibid., 70–71.

19. Ibid., 72.

20. Ibid., 72.

CHAPTER 10

1. Senate Committee on Foreign Relations, *Controlling Space Weapons*, S. Hrg. 98–141, 98th Cong., 1st Sess., April 14, 1983, 30 (hereinafter cited as *Controlling Space Weapons*).

2. Senate Committee on Armed Services, *Department of Defense Authorization for Appropriations for Fiscal Year 1984*, S. Hrg. 98–49, Part 5, 98th Cong., 1st Sess., May 2, 1983, 2904–5.

3. Senate Committee on Foreign Relations, Subcommittee on Arms Control, Oceans, International Operations, and Environment, *Arms Control and the Militarization of Space*, Hearing on S. Res. 129, 97th Cong., 2d Sess., September 20, 1982, 37.

4. Senate Committee on Foreign Relations, *Strategic Defense and Anti-Satellite Weapons*, S. Hrg. 98–750, 98th Cong., 2d Sess., April 25, 1984, 145–46 (hereinafter cited as *Anti-Satellite Weapons*).

5. Ibid., 164.

6. Ibid., 148, 150–51, 153–56, 162–63.

7. Ibid., 201–4.

8. Ibid., 322.

9. Ibid., 350.

10. Ibid., 355.

11. House Committee on Armed Services, Subcommittee on Research and Development and Subcommittee on Investigations, *H.R. 3073, People Protection Act*, H.A.S.C. 98–21, 98th Cong., 1st Sess., November 10, 1983, 21–22.

12. *Anti-Satellite Weapons*, 74–75.

13. Ibid., 75.

14. Ibid., 75–77.

15. Ibid., 179.

16. Excerpts from Dr. Jastrow's testimony are taken from House Republican Study Committee, *The Strategic Defense Initiative: Deterring War and Defending Mankind*, 98th Cong., 2d Sess., August 9, 1984, appendix.

17. *Controlling Space Weapons*, 47–48.

18. Ibid., 48–49.

19. Ibid., 49–50.

20. Senate Committee on Armed Services, *Department of Defense Authorization for Appropriations for Fiscal Year 1984*, March 23, 1983, 2668–69.

CHAPTER 11

1. *Washington Post*, March 1, 1985, A13.

2. Congressional delegation led by Senate Majority Leader Robert Dole (R-Kans.) to the European countries of England, France, Germany, and Italy during April 5–13, 1985.

3. Speech to the Bundestag, Bonn, West Germany, April 18, 1985.

4. *New York Times*, December 23, 1984, 1, 13.

5. *Washington Post*, December 23, 1984, 1.

6. Farooq Hussain, "Will Space Weapons Sink Britain's Trident Fleet?" *New Scientist* 105 (January 3, 1985): 8.

7. Sir Geoffrey Howe, "Defence and Security in the Nuclear Age," Text of speech delivered on March 15, 1985, to the Royal United Services Institute, London, England. Press release of text by British Embassy in Washington, D.C.

8. *Washington Post*, March 21, 1985, A15.

9. *World Opinion Update*, March 1985, 9 (9): 28–29.

10. U.S. Library of Congress. Congressional Research Service. *The Strategic Defense Initiative and United States Alliance Strategy*. Report 85–48F, by Paul E. Gallis, Mark M. Lowenthal, and Marcia S. Smith, February 1, 1985 (continually updated). Washington, 1985, 43.

11. Ibid., 44.

12. *Washington Post*, February 10, 1985, 1, 27.

13. Ibid., April 24, 1985, 127–28.

14. *Washington Times*, April 19, 1985, 4A.

15. For example, Monique Garnier-Loncon, "Star Wars," *Aviation 2000*, April 1985, 29–33. Garnier-Loncon is a deputy mayor of Paris and vice-president of the European Institute of Security. See also François de Rose, "Wars: The Weapons Are Forever Changing," *Le Nouvel Observateur*, November 2, 1984, 63.

16. *New York Times*, March 29, 1985, A–9; *Wall Street Journal*, March 29, 1985, 32.

17. *Washington Post*, April 19, 1985, A–30.

18. *New York Times*, April 24, 1985, A–5.

19. *Washington Post*, April 24, 1985, A–27.

20. Ibid., May 5, 1985, 1, 24.

21. Ibid., May 23, 1985, A29.

22. Ibid., May 29, 1985, A26.

23. Ibid., June 3, 1985, A16.

24. Joseph Gambardello, "NATO Ministers Support U.S. Positions at Geneva," United Press International, June 7, 1985; *New York Times*, "NATO Now Cooler to Space Weapons," June 7, 1985, A10.

Bibliography

De Rose, François. "Wars: The Weapons Are Forever Changing." *Le Nouvel Observateur*, November 2, 1984, p. 63.

Dewar, Helen. "Anti-Satellite Tests Backed, with Condition." *Washington Post*, June 13, 1984, p. A–9.

Eisenhower, Dwight D. "Address before the General Assembly of the United Nations on Peaceful Uses of Atomic Energy," December 8, 1953. In *Public Papers of the Presidents of the United States*. Washington, D.C.: U.S. Government Printing Office, 1953.

Gambardello, Joseph. "NATO Ministers Support U.S. Positions at Geneva." United Press International, June 7, 1985.

Garnier-Loncon, Monique. "Star Wars." *Aviation 2000*, April 1985, pp. 29–33.

Howe, Sir Geoffrey. "Defence and Security in the Nuclear Age." Text of speech delivered on March 15, 1985, to the Royal United Services Institute (London, England).

Hussain, Farooq. "Will Space Weapons Sink Britain's Trident Fleet?" *New Scientist*, Vol. 105, January 3, 1985, p. 8.

Kohl, Helmut. Speech to the Bundestag, Bonn, West Germany, April 18, 1985.

Nixon, Richard. "Statement on Deployment of the Anti-Ballistic Missile System," March 14, 1969. In *Public Papers of the Presidents of the United States*. Washington, D.C.: U.S. Government Printing Office, 1969.

Reagan, Ronald. "Defense Spending and Defensive Technology." In *Weekly Compilation of Presidential Documents*, Vol. 19, March 23, 1983, pp. 423–66.

Smith, R. Jeffrey. "Aerospace Experts Challenge ASAT Decision." *Science*, Vol. 224, May 18, 1984, pp. 693–96.

U.S. Arms Control and Disarmament Agency. *Arms Control and Disarmament Agreements: Texts and Histories of Negotiations*. Washington, D.C.: U.S. Government Printing Office, 1982.

U.S. Congress. Congressional Research Service. *Space Shuttle*, by Marcia S. Smith. Issue Brief 1B81175, February 19, 1985, pp. 8–9.

_____. Congressional Research Service. *Star Wars: Antisatellites and Space-Based BMD*, by Marcia S. Smith. Issue Brief IB81123, February 20, 1985, pp. 2–7, 12.

_____. Congressional Research Service. *The Strategic Defense Initiative and United States Alliance Strategy*, by Paul E. Gallis, Mark M. Lowenthal, and Marcia S. Smith. Report 85–48 F, February 1, 1985, p. 43.

_____. House. 98th Cong., 1st Sess., March 24, April 7, May 26, and June 14, 1983. *Congressional Record*, Vol. 129.

_____. House. 98th Cong., 2d Sess., May 23 and 24, 1984. *Congressional Record*, Vol. 130.

_____ . House. 99th Cong., 1st Sess., May 15 and June 20, 24, and 26, 1985. *Congressional Record*, Vol. 131.

_____ . House. Committee on Appropriations. *Hearings before the Subcommittee on Defense of the House Committee on Appropriations on Department of Defense Appropriations for 1984*, 98th Cong., 1st Sess., 1983.

_____ . House. Committee on Appropriations. *Hearings before the Subcommittee on Defense of the House Committee on Appropriations on Department of Defense Appropriations for 1985*, 98th Cong., 2d Sess., 1984.

_____ . House. Committee on Armed Services. *Hearings before the House Committee on Armed Services on Defense Department Authorization and Oversight*, 98th Cong., 1st Sess., 1983.

_____ . House. Committee on Armed Services. *Hearings before the House Committee on Armed Services on Defense Department Authorization and Oversight*, 98th Cong., 2d Sess., 1984.

_____ . House. Committee on Armed Services. *Hearings before the Subcommittee on Research and Development and the Subcommittee on Investigations of the House Committee on Armed Services on H.R. 3073, People Protection Act*, 98th Cong., 1st Sess., 1983.

_____ . House. Committee on Foreign Affairs. *Arms Control in Outer Space. Hearings before the Subcommittee on International Security and Scientific Affairs of the House Committee on Foreign Affairs*, 98th Cong., 2d Sess., 1984.

_____ . House. Committee on Foreign Affairs. *The Role of Arms Control in U.S. Defense Policy. Hearings before the House Committee on Foreign Affairs*, 98th Cong., 2d Sess., 1984.

_____ . House. Republican Study Committee. *The Strategic Defense Initiative: Deterring War and Defending Mankind. Hearings before the House Republican Study Committee*, 98th Cong., 2d Sess., 1984.

_____ . Office of Technology Assessment. *Arms Control in Space: Workshop Proceedings*. Washington, D.C.: U.S. Government Printing Office, May 1984, p. 43.

_____ . Senate. 98th Cong., 1st Sess., February 2 and 3 and July 14 and 18, 1983. *Congressional Record*. Vol. 129.

_____ . Senate. 98th Cong., 2d Sess., May 23, June 12, 13, 19, and 26 and October 3, 1984. *Congressional Record*, Vol. 130.

_____ . Senate. 99th Cong., 1st Sess., May 17 and 24 and June 3, 4, and 5, 1985. *Congressional Record*, Vol. 131.

_____ . Senate. Committee on Appropriations. *Department of Defense Appropriations, FY 85. Hearings before the Subcommittee on Defense Appropriations of the Senate Committee on Appropriations*, 98th Cong., 2d Sess., 1984.

_____ . Senate. Committee on Armed Services. *Department of Defense Authorization for Appropriations for Fiscal Year 1984. Hearings before the Senate Committee on Armed Services*, 98th Cong., 1st Sess., 1983.

_____. Senate. Committee on Armed Services. *Department of Defense Authorization for Appropriations for Fiscal Year 1985. Hearings before the Senate Committee on Armed Services*, 98th Cong., 2d Sess., 1984.

_____. Senate. Committee on Foreign Relations. *Arms Control Overview. Hearing before the Senate Committee on Foreign Relations*, 98th Cong., 2d Sess., 1984.

_____. Senate. Committee on Foreign Relations. *Arms Control and the Militarization of Space. Hearings before the Subcommittee on Arms Control, Oceans, International Operations, and Environment of the Senate Committee on Foreign Relations*, 97th Cong., 2d Sess., 1982.

_____. Senate. Committee on Foreign Relations. *Controlling Space Weapons. Hearing before the Senate Committee on Foreign Relations*, 98th Cong., 1st Sess., 1983.

_____. Senate. Committee on Foreign Relations. *East–West Cooperation in Outer Space. Hearing before the Senate Foreign Relations Committee*, 98th Cong., 2d Sess., 1984.

_____. Senate. Committee on Foreign Relations. *Nomination of Kenneth L. Adelman. Hearing before the Senate Committee on Foreign Relations*, 98th Cong., 1st Sess., 1983.

_____. Senate. Committee on Foreign Relations. *Outer Space Arms Control Negotiations. Hearing before the Senate Committee on Foreign Relations*, 98th Cong., 1st Sess., 1983.

_____. Senate. Committee on Foreign Relations. *The SALT II Treaty. Hearing before the Senate Committee on Foreign Relations*, 96th Cong., 2d Sess., 1979.

_____. Senate. Committee on Foreign Relations. *Strategic Defense and Anti-Satellite Weapons. Hearing before the Senate Committee on Foreign Relations*, 98th Cong., 2d Sess., 1984.

_____. Senate. Committee on Foreign Relations. *United States–Soviet Relations. Hearing before the Senate Committee on Foreign Relations*, 98th Cong., 1st Sess., 1983.

U.S. Department of Defense. *Report to the Congress on the Strategic Defense Initiative*, 1985.

_____. *Soviet Military Power 1985*. 4th ed. Washington, D.C.: U.S. Government Printing Office, 1985.

U.S. Department of State. *Treaties in Force: A List of Treaties and Other International Agreements of the United States in Force on January 1, 1985*. Pubn. No. 9433. Washington, D.C.: U.S. Government Printing Office, 1985.

White House. *Report to the Congress on U.S. Policy on ASAT Arms Control*, March 31, 1984.

World Opinion Update, Vol. 9, March 1985, pp. 28–29.

Index

About the Author

U.S. Senator Larry Pressler (R-S.D.) served as Chairman of the Senate Foreign Relations Subcommittee on Arms Control 1981 to 1985. He is the current Chairman of the Subcommittee on European Affairs. He also serves on the Senate Commerce, Science, and Transportation Committee, Senate Small Business Committee, and Senate Special Committee on Aging. First elected to the House of Representatives in 1974, he was elected to the Senate in 1978 and reelected in 1984. Pressler earned a Diploma, Oxford (England) University and M.A. and J.D. degrees from Harvard University and Harvard Law School, respectively. His B.A. degree is from the University of South Dakota, where he won Phi Beta Kappa honors. He served in Vietnam as a lieutenant in the U.S. Army.

NCC LIBRARY

a34011 041378230b

Everett Baker
Learning Resources Center
NORWALK COMMUNITY COLLEGE